Contents

Introduction

There are still many spectacular, wild and rarely visited places in the Far North, despite the best efforts of developers to wreck the area, first with huge swathes of useless forestry and now with even more useless and intrusive wind-farms. Even local people are often unaware of the amazing places and wildlife so close to their back doors. Caithness and Sutherland boast the finest coastal, mountain and moorland scenery in Britain and there are few comparable locations in the world. In Caithness alone you can see otters and wildcats and pine martens, you can listen to the red-deer stags in rut and look down to grey seal colonies on inaccessible beaches. There are foxes and badgers and short-eared owls and hen-harriers, there are the wildly wailing divers on flow-country dubh-lochs, there are the mournful calls of greenshank and golden plover, there are huge flocks of migrating geese. Some of the high cliffs become spectacular sea-bird cities in the spring and early summer, thronged with kittiwakes and guillemots and razorbills with puffins in clifftop burrows and shags on slabby rocks near the sea. Above all is the big dome of the sky and the weather which can often be dramatic in both summer and winter.

This is first and foremost a picture book. If, like me, you never begin a book at page one, have a quick flick through. Then enjoy it at a more leisurely pace. I hope you also enjoy reading my stories of journeying through the remotest north by sea-kayak, on foot and by bike, some of which are based on my outdoor column in the *Caithness Courier* – Out and About with Ralph.

I would not call myself a photographer. All the pictures in this book were taken with compact digital cameras. I've never, ever used a SLR (whatever that is) with a tripod. My great advantage lies in getting into places and in weather conditions where real photographers never venture. Only a couple of the 300 or so photos in the book were taken from a road and few of the remainder were composed while on a path or beaten trail. Real photographers don't kayak through the sea-caves into Wifie Geo, or cross the Knockfin Heights on bike or skis. Real photographers like to spend a long time setting up a picture and so often miss the lighting conditions you can get so briefly out of doors which a basic camera, quickly drawn from the pocket or life-jacket, can record.

The counties are a wonderful place to enjoy walking, cycling, sea-kayaking, running or even just pottering round the little harbours with a car. Unlike some areas such as the English Lake District which flaunt their beauties for all to see, the wonders of Caithness and Sutherland are often more shy and need to be looked for off the beaten track.

And that is what this book does. It takes you well off the beaten track in the Far North and gives a flavour of what can be found if you just go out and explore.

Ralph

Ralph's Secret North

Ralph MacGregor

Curlew Cottage Books

Published by
Curlew Cottage Books
Curlew Cottage,
Hilliclay Mains,
Weydale, Thurso
Caithness KW14 8YN

© text and photographs 2013 Ben Ralph MacGregor

ISBN 978-0-9538703-3-2

All rights reserved.
No part of this publication may be reproduced,
stored in a retrieval system, or transmitted,
in any form or by any means, electronic, mechanical or otherwise
without prior permission of the publisher

Typeset by Ben MacGregor
Printed and bound by Bell & Bain Ltd

Chapter 1   No Grey Coast!

From Helmsdale to Wick

An Dun

A mystery beckoned. Mist clung to the tops of dark cliffs, drizzle and rain spotted from time to time onto the oily-calm sea at Dunbeath. Let me quote from Calder's 1887 'History of Caithness'; Calder himself is quoting a tourist visiting Dunbeath Castle around 1783.

'Underneath the castle is a large cavern running up from the sea... from within the castle the approach to this dismal place is by steps cut in the rock, formed like a narrow stair, twisting round and round as it descends into the vault. The entry to this stair is curiously covered from the sight of those who are not acquainted with it...'

Strangely I have found nobody, native of Dunbeath or otherwise, who can vouch whether or not this story is true. There is certainly no obvious entrance to a stairway leading from the castle. The owner insists the stairs are there but that the entrance was cemented up many years ago to prevent rats and 'other vermin' from climbing up from the sea. A lady who used to work in the castle told me that a certain doorway led to the stairs, but she never saw the door unlocked. Another story is that there is a secret door behind a big picture near the main entrance.

From the beach by the harbour I kayaked across the grey, gently rippling water. In little more than ten minutes I

was below the castle and could see a narrow slot of a cave running into the rocky headland on which the white buildings of the castle stand. In the gentle swell I paddled up to the mouth of the cave, a passage led inwards between narrowing rock walls with suggestions of a boulder beach at the end. In the grey, early morning light it didn't seem the friendliest of places with the sound of sloshing water and breaking waves echoing outwards. No, it didn't appeal at all.

After a few hours of exploring that amazing coast south to Berriedale I was back. The wind was still very light, with a smir of rain, on approaching Dunbeath Castle again. I'd have another look at that cave. Emboldened by my other explorations I now noticed that it was possible to carefully paddle in backwards, helped by the small swell that was washing in. Cautiously feeling my way between the rock walls – it wasn't quite as narrow as it looked – I backed into the gloom. Yes, there was a little beach of rounded, seaweedy boulders, the boat grounded and I clambered out and hauled it up out of

Berriedale Harbour

reach of the swell...

Most people have no idea just how spectacular the Caithness coast is. Many will know Dunnet Bay or Reiss Bay, some will have visited the tiny harbours of Latheronwheel or Harrow or Auckengill. The rest, they think, is just bleak grey cliffs. Let me try to convince you otherwise!

On a gloriously fine day between weathers I went to explore what to me is well known country. The coast from Helmsdale to Dunbeath is, like much of the coastline, of the best. The little harbour at Berriedale is itself a lovely spot, with kittiwakes calling from ledges on the cliff just above the last, deep, river pool. It must be one of the few places where people can watch nesting kittiwakes from their bedroom window. The tide was in, so I launched the sea-kayak in the pool and paddled straight out into the low breaking waves. It was a perfect morning of clear blue sky and views across the sea to the distant snow-covered Cairngorms – but cold! The wind was forecast to pick up from the south-east by evening as another bout of wet and windy weather approached,

so to be on the safe side I planned to be out of the water by early afternoon and then do a bit of exploring on foot.

It wasn't far to the big colonies of sea-birds, the kittiwakes already in place but the razorbills and guillemots still selecting their nesting spots on the narrow cliff ledges like arrays of little soldiers. Not yet settled, the lines of black-and-white birds would take off if

the boat came too close, hurtling towards the sea with rapidly beating wings. One misjudged it and hit the boat with a considerable thump. I always carry a helmet, to put on if attempting a surf landing or maybe if venturing into sea caves or practicing rolling in shallows. Now I donned it for protection from low-flying birds as another array of black-and-white

High cliffs of the Ord

missiles hurtled past, narrowly missing me to splash into the water.

The day continued with clear unbroken sunshine and little choppy waves giving for a glorious paddle down the spectacular coast with the air full of sea-birds and their calls sounding from the cliff ledges. Black shags perched on low rocks above the water or flew holding strands of grass and seaweed to partly-built nests, splashing into the sea if I came too near when exploring shallow sea-caves.

The reddish cliffs rise to 400 feet but are more broken and less austere than those further north. Ever so often there is an enticing stony beach to land on and explore. Here is a hillside of huge tumbled boulders, there are stacks and skerries and rocks to paddle in and out of. Here too, about a mile west of Berriedale, is the sharp rock stack known variously as 'The Needle' or 'Bodach an Uird' (The old man of the Ord). Often seen from a distance when looking along the coastline to the Ord, the only easy way of getting close to it is from the sea.

Towards Ousdale I paddled under cliffs below Badbea, where folk had to settle in the nineteenth century on the exposed steep slopes after being cleared from the sheltered inland straths. There are one or two difficult routes to the shore from the old houses but no decent sites for launching boats.

The Ousdale burn comes down to the sea at a delightful little boulder-bay over a waterfall between cliffs. There is no way up or down without rock-climbing, the only access to this bay is from the sea. You can land knowing that only a handful of people have set foot here in recent years, although no more than a mile from the A9.

The inaccessible Ousdale Bay

Looking out from Ousdale Bay

Out on the sea again I carried on round the next headland to where the cliffs run out onto the stony shores of St. Ninians Bay leading to Helmsdale, then with the wind and sea beginning to pick up, turned. There's no hardship in paddling back the same way, there are different caves and bays to explore. Back at Berriedale I sorted out gear in the sunshine then set off to visit some favourite spots on foot.

Between Berriedale and Dunbeath is the high stack of An Dun, joined to the mainland by a narrow bridge over a huge sea arch. Under steep grassy slopes the cliffs drop sheer or overhanging for two or three hundred feet, with some of the largest colonies of guillemots and razorbills in the county. No ranger-

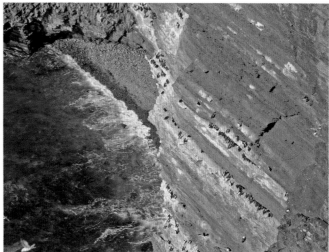

those deceptively green slopes are huge drops all round. And then there are the sheep. The fences which used to keep them off are broken, and it is almost heart-stopping to see the fearless animals, some of them big with lamb, scampering along narrow trods above hundreds of feet of thin air. I know they fall off, I've found the remains on the inaccessible beaches below.

Let me just say that one of the most amazing places on the whole east coast lies somewhere between Dunbeath and Helmsdale. The sheep have been kept out for many years but all it would take

guided walks come here, you need to be sure-footed with a good head for heights! Indeed the top of An Dun has that unsettling feel to it you find on the exposed tops of the Cuillin, just beyond

A hillside of wild garlic

This high waterfall lies between Berriedale and Dunbeath

to wreck the place would be to let them in. There are two boulder-bays and a sea-stack, seemingly inaccessible from the land. Look more closely and a way down to the first bay, 300 feet below, appears. The remains of an old path zigzags down sunny slopes covered in primroses. Here too in early May is red campion, a first orchid, spikes of blue bugle, purple violets, yellow celandine. Twenty years ago a landslip removed the path, further descent is only for the experienced hill-walker. Carefully rounding loose broken crags another steep green slope leads down to the sea, an entire acre of 45-degree hillside covered in a luscious growth of wild garlic with its white flowers in full bloom. Down at the bay with the tide out, it's possible to walk across the boulders and rocks to the stack and then right round to the second bay, which can normally only be reached by sea. At the back of this bay is an enormous overhang with a small cave leading further in. Low stone walls show that this place was, once, known and used.

I made my way slowly back up as bees buzzed and an early tortoishell butterfly fluttered over the flowery slopes, the wind was cold but these east coast hillsides are a suntrap.

I'm told that some flowers grow here that are found nowhere else in the county. A little bit of heaven, still miraculously unspoilt in spite of being so near the road – long may it remain so.

Another morning, another month. Dawn is coming up, it's just after nine in

early January and already I've been walking for over an hour from Latheronwheel Harbour, following the coast north-eastwards in a cold rising wind and increasing cloud. Having left the car a bit up the road from the

Sea-kayaks at Dunbeath

A sea cave near Dunbeath

harbour (to avoid it getting drenched by spray), I rounded the point by means of an awkward scramble below the fence – it's easier to go further inland – and reached the top of cliffs above a long, stony beach stretching eastwards. Halfway along, an easy grassy slope led down giving a chance to explore. Now, climbing back up at the end of the bay and avoiding some very dodgy loose rock, I find myself immediately above a slope leading down to the Latheron Burn. A very steep descent by the fence takes me to another small stony beach –

then straight up again, picking a way through gorse to the top of Red Point with yet another bay stretching out in front. It's slightly above freezing, a raw east wind, some spray and spume but the sea choppy rather than really rough. The sun is just rising over the sea under the edge of a sheet of red cloud spreading in from the west. A true sailors' warning morning...

Ten minutes later. I've scrambled down to the big bay, the rising sun has now gone behind the sheet of cloud. Another nice stony shoreline, a little

sand, ancient driftwood, lots of the old blue containers which have littered this coast for years. There's a dead guillemot, nothing obvious wrong with it, just dead.

Nine-thirty. I'm at the next bay, an easy scramble across slippery rocks but you wouldn't get round at high tide. Loads of driftwood, some very long tree trunks. A couple of fulmars on a cliff ledge look as if they're already staking out nesting sites. At the far end of this beach I'll probably have to climb up again, should be steep but easy. In the

Dawn at Latheronwheel

The Latheron beaches

Sea stack near Dunbeath

middle of the bay there's a little waterfall, this is a lovely spot on a sunny morning a bit later in the year.

Nine-forty. The steep slopes up from the bay were thickly grown with gorse, I had to be careful picking a route to avoid getting tangled up in it. Then easy walking along the clifftop, climbing a low wall, to what looks like an old lookout. Solid stone, square, eight feet tall, with steps to the top. To the south the Clan Gunn Centre, the cemetery and the old bell-tower above Latheron – I'll pass that on the way back – with Scaraben in the distance looking bleak with a few streaks of snow against the grey sky. I can see the lorries on the A9, it's strange that this stretch of coast near the road is so wild and almost unexplored.

Five minutes later. That was silly, I've scrambled down to the next bay and discovered I could easily have made my way round the point without having to climb up, only at high tide is the route barred. But then I'd have missed seeing that odd lookout. Anyway I'm now going to follow the shore, I should be able to get quite a way along.

Forse Bay

Ten-twenty. I'm at the far end of the beach, below a stack, some very interesting contorted rocks here and the odd fossil. Some recent rock falls. Spray and spume blowing from the breaking waves. There's no way on, I'll have to climb up the very steep grass.

Ten-thirty-five. I'm on the clifftop approaching another small waterfall completely blown back in the now gale-force wind. Under the fall the rocks look dry! It's an easy walk along the top by the wall, but a very buffeting wind, the sky now totally grey, a typical dark January day.

Ten-forty. Below the falls, is a little bay, Port na Muic, which I'd completely forgotten about, easy to get down by a very steep descent over grass, perhaps traces of an old zigzag path. There's a mass of detritus on the beach including three footballs and loads more of those blue plastic containers. You can get right to the bottom of the waterfall when the tide is low, this is a spectacular spot when there's a lot of water about.

Eleven-fifteen. Now at Forse Falls. It was quite difficult to get along the top of the cliffs, first drenched by the backwards-blowing waterfall then with the rising wind, now at least force nine, trying to pin me against the barbed-wire fence. I didn't attempt to venture out onto the narrow promontories. Just short of the falls is a geo which was easy to scramble down and, with the tide low, I could walk round to the Forss Burn below the falls, cross the burn and climb up the other side.

Eleven-thirty and a walk along a narrow ridge between the Forss Burn and the next big bay. I crossed the fence for safety and enjoyed easy walking along the field above the burn with its little-known native woodland. Ahead, a flock of hungry sheep are eyeing my rucksac hopefully. There's a well-constructed stone seat here, right by the fence, overlooking an increasingly

Achastle Castle

stormy Forse bay − another steep, but easy descent. By the time I've finished this walk I'll have done more climbing and descending than required for many a Munro!

Twelve-forty-five. I'm sitting out of the gale by the ruined croft of Achnacraig on Swiney Hill above Lybster. The people who lived here had a fantastic view, right out across the sea. It's a typical Caithness ruin, windows gone, a few old armchairs, fallen plaster and broken glass, wind howling around and through. (It's probably all changed here now with oil-related developments, I've not felt like going back to look.)

Overlooking Lybster bay is a viewpoint, a seat with drawings by the local primary school children inscribed in the concrete, a good view of the waves breaking over the harbour wall in clouds of spray with a very grey Lybster village beyond. I'm now going to make my way back inland across the fields and moors to Latheronwheel, the sky looks dark and threatening, the gale will soon dissolve into rain.

Three-thirty. I'm back at Latheronwheel, the rain didn't come to much and the sun even appeared briefly to set behind low cloud to the south, illuminating the bay below in lovely sunset light as it did. I found quite a good route back, the only awkward bit being the crossing of the deep burn cut between Achastle and Burrigill.

Now let's take to the sea again. To paddle a sea-kayak from Lybster to Wick in a day makes quite a long trip of around 20 miles, I had to be fit enough to attempt it! So some practice in safer water first.

'The time has come, the Walrus said...' I could prevaricate no longer. The sun was bright but the waters of Loch Calder, which had been frozen only a few weeks earlier, were cold. There were one or two anglers, in boat or on the shore, hopeful or maybe, like me, just practicing − surely no self-

Razorbills

Loch Calder

respecting fly would be hatching in these conditions.

I'd ventured out, wet-suit clad, to get wet. Could I still 'roll' the boat upright after capsizing? A skill I can manage easily in the swimming pool in a play 'Polo' boat, even with a polystyrene float instead of a paddle. But it's a lot harder outdoors in a long sea-kayak. I threw myself over, the icy water numbing my ears which were still tender after a cold. My roll was not the most elegant but I made it back upright. And a second time. To try a third time, or on the 'other' side, would be tempting fate.

And so I paddled on, enjoying my first circuit of the year of Loch Calder. Below the still-bare woods of the

Shieling, past the chambered cairn and broch, along the remote western shore and out round the marshy islands to the south, as greylags called from the middle of the loch. Occasionally I'd stop to try another roll, failing once, enough to warn me that I still couldn't rely on it. Just keep practicing... it will be easier when the waters warm up!

Having managed the six miles with little bother I reckoned I was up for the long trip, it was only April but a forecast of very light winds and calm seas was too good to miss. So on a fine morning of sunshine, frost and a little drifting mist I unloaded the boat at Lybster harbour, drove up to Wick and caught the friendly bus back to Lybster. It seems such a short way by road, no more than 20 minutes. Yet below is an amazing 15 miles of contorted cliffs, geos, sea-stacks, caves, skerries... This whole coast would have been intimately known in the past when the sea was the livelihood of those who lived here. Look at a large scale map; every feature is named. Now, only a few creel fishermen preserve that familiarity with this austere coastline.

Clyth Falls

Although a big of area high pressure was sitting over Caithness, a very weak front promised grey skies later with a possibility of a bit more wind, the forecast assured no more than force three but I had my doubts. My main concern was sore tendons in the arms, either due to old age or maybe brought on by the previous day of planting trees in the wood and tatties in the garden. My working life was mostly spent at a desk, and it shows. I could though always turn back to Lybster, or get out at Sarclet. Or even Whaligoe. But things would have to be really bad before I'd consider dragging the boat up

North-east of Lybster

A fine cave near Occumster

those 350 or so steps!

I headed out from the beach below the visitor centre into gently rippling seas and sunshine, rounding the point and soon paddling though the first little sea cave of the day. With approaching 20 miles to go, I'd have to be selective about exploring the caves and geos, but some were just too good to miss.

It is hard to describe just how spectacular this Caithness coastline is. Feature after feature which, if moved to the coast of England, would be famous on calendars and tourist advertisements, but here are just another sea-cave or natural arch or towering stack. All along the cliffs there were kittiwakes. I don't think there was one minute between Lybster Bay and South Head when the air was not echoing with 'Kitt-ee wake, kitt-ee-wake'. The white birds with the dipped-in-black-ink wingtips were already ensconced on nests of mud and dead grass, squeezed onto the cliff ledges. Numbers have declined greatly in recent years, these cliffs must have been an incredible sight in the past. On the water were small rafts of black guillemots with their white wing patches and red feet, they would fly off towards the cliffs with little peeping calls. The squawking of common guillemots on lower cliff ledges also filled the air, with the constant sound of the swell washing into the towering cliffs. There was the smell of seaweed and salt and guano, there was the steady paddling rhythm, the occasional rush of cold water against the hands. Having tender tendons was no bad thing, it

meant I had to adopt a good paddling style where the arms are kept straight and most of the work is done by rotating the body. I reckoned I'd last the distance.

North of Lybster you paddle a narrow passage between a stack and cliffs with sloping rock strata dipping into the sea; the illusion of going steeply downhill is disorientatingly strong and some concentration is required to negotiate rocks at the end of the channel. On a foggy day this area has a Tolkeinesque feel to it with cliffs and huge stacks rising into the mist and long, mysterious geos fading into the gloom. I passed Occumster Bay, with its ruined herring building and fine cave nearby, I passed Clyth Harbour with its waterfall

and hillside access shelf, I watched the seals take to the water from Black Skerry and Skerry Mor, I paddled below a sunlit mid-Clyth lighthouse. One seal was dozing in the water, I was about to take a photo from a few feet away when it turned, saw me and dived with a panicked splash, the camera recording nothing but white water.

The cliffs become their darkest and most austere approaching Whaligoe, here are Hanni Geo and the Haven, old flights of steps which preceded Whaligoe and gave access to these little rocky harbours prominently seen from the boat. A great thing about the kayak is the ability it gives to explore close in to rocks and to navigate shallow water and narrow passages which bigger boats have to avoid. Below Bruan are the most forbidding and black of cliffs with deep geos, nothing pretty about the place and yet amazingly close to the road and the two old Bruan churches. A sea-cave at the back of the biggest geo runs in a long way, probably right under the old buildings. Indeed, paddling for hours up this coast, I was never more than a mile from the A99 but could have been in the

Whaligoe Coast

Whaligoe Steps

Whaligoe

depths of wilderness. The only signs of human life I saw on the whole trip were a single distant creel boat and a digger incongruously parked on the clifftops near Ulbster where a new fence was being erected.

A long, narrow sea-cave leads right through the headland into Wester Whale Geo, it seemed that the sun was shining when I entered the cave and the skies were grey when I came out. I paddled on round into Whaligoe and beached the boat, a rare chance to visit this spectacular spot without climbing down and up the 350 steps! Just north of Whaligoe, at the mouth of a big cave, the outflow from Loch Watenan tumbles some 200 feet vertically into the sea, you can paddle right under the waterfall.

Sarclet, another three miles up the coast, would be the next place where I could easily land. Under grey skies I carried on north, paddling into long narrow geos under towering black walls, through sea-caves and channels between sea-stacks, so much scenery blurring together in the memory. The weather was deteriorating as expected, nothing to worry about but now a few spots of drizzle and it looked like the last miles up to Wick would be into a headwind of force three or four, negating the favourable tide. I'd got into

Sarclet

Brig O' Tram

Dunbar's Stack

Stack of Ulbster

The Needle

'Scorries Island'

a good rhythm and passed Sarclet, carrying on by Riera Geo with its high waterfall, past Broad Geo and Todd's Geo before finally rounding the headland and paddling into Ires Geo to land the boat among slippery rocks for another much-needed tea-break. At the mouth of this geo is one of the highlights of the trip, the huge natural arch of 'The Needle' with a smaller 'Needle's Eye' just above the water level. Beyond is a giant, cathedral-like sea cave which could swallow any of our churches. There were still miles to go

and I was tiring, this is a coast to enjoy on a fine day and a bit bleak in sheeting drizzle. I kept close in to the cliffs, both for shelter and to enjoy the bird colonies and caves, even though it meant paddling further. Geo after geo, headland after headland. At last – the Stack of Brough, known locally as Scorries Island. Another of the amazing features of this amazing coast, this has a huge hole in the middle, prominently seen from planes taking off from Wick airport. A sea-cave some 200 yards long runs longways through the stack, to

paddle this passage, gazing up at the sky halfway along (alas no passing plane to wave to) was perhaps the main highlight of the trip.

It was a slog into the wind and drizzle for the last couple of miles, knowing though that there were plenty of safe places to land as I passed the Grey Bouls – impossibly huge boulders thrown up by a colossal storm in centuries past – and paddled on by the slabby rocks of the Trinkie to finally round South Head and cross the bay to the river mouth. The tide was out, the

last effort of the day was to drag the boat up the river to the slipway at the Camps. It was after five, an ordinary grey afternoon in the grey town. Even Wick has mostly turned its back on the sea which once sustained it, everywhere were towny people doing towny things. As I queued at the Co-op checkout on the way home, the trip already seemed like a dream. Only a sore wrist and a boat dripping sand and sea-water all over the car proved I'd actually completed my longest sea-paddle.

So, back to that mysterious cave under Dunbeath Castle... Twenty feet above, a high roof. The narrow cave climbed into darkness beyond the beach, the ground covered in the usual detritus of old fishing floats, bits of net

and broken boat. I scrambled up, glad of my helmet as it cracked against a jutting rock. Oh for a torch, I hadn't expected to be able to explore in here. Now it was too dark to see what lay beyond. There seemed to be metal projecting from the wall – an old ladder perhaps? And that passage continued on, and up... but on my own with no light I was not going any further.

It was a couple of years before I was back, this time better equipped with a torch. Now I could see that the metal was twisted bits of old boat, partly buried in boulders. Scrambling up over this, the torch revealed a narrowing cave coming to a dead end above steeply rising piled stones. No sign a t all of any stair, blocked up or otherwise. The high roof of the cave looked precarious, with old plastic floats and other debris wedged into it.

I'm skeptical that there ever was a flight of steps. A geo, just to the east, would give much easier secluded access to the castle via a steep grassy bank. But any entrance could well be buried under that piled rubble from the storms of centuries. Would some digging uncover

a doorway to a secret, spiral stairway leading up into the darkness to emerge, perhaps, in a forgotten, walled-off cellar? Nobody seems to know.

The Caithness coast is like that. Go and explore!

Chapter 2 Headlands and Bays

From Wick to Strathy Point

Strathy Bay

The coastline from Wick, round Noss Head, Duncansby Head and Dunnet Head to Thurso then on west to Strathy Point and Armadale is one of one of the finest in the world. A coast of fierce tide-races, high cliffs, geos, stacks and sea-caves, magnificent sandy beaches, inaccessible coves and low rocky shorelines with great slabs of sandstone rock. Every few miles there's an old castle, sometimes ruinous, sometimes renovated. There are seals, otters, whales, porpoises and huge colonies of cliff-nesting birds.

A little snowman, or rather snow bird, sat on our bird table for a few hours scaring the starlings away after a rare mid-October snowfall. And only five months since another garden snowman incongruously kept company with the tulips in mid-May. Well, global warming or no, I refused to accept that Summer was yet over.

So the next morning, admiring the early sunshine and ignoring the car thermometer which read -2C on the way to Keiss, I unloaded the boat from the roof for a trip along the bay to

Ackergill. With a gentle swell, a light following wind and a helping tide it promised to be a lazy journey, after which I'd jog back down the beach to collect the car.

Indeed sun-dazzle proved the only hazard, with little effort I cruised along just seawards of the breaking surf, listening to the roar of the waves on the empty sands. Towards Ackergill I practiced some gentle surfing, riding in on the waves then paddling back out through the surf before landing on the sands in the glorious morning sunshine.

Noss Head

Sunset at Keiss

Reiss Beach

A man out walking his dog was surprised to meet a kayaker, it was, he said, very rare to see anybody paddling here. Where else would such a fine beach not be thronged with people!

At Ackergill harbour I pulled the boat up onto the grass and changed into light running clothes for an hour or so's easy run back to Keiss. I'd checked the winds and tides for the paddle – but had forgotten that at high tide much of the sand would now be underwater. First, I had to scramble along walls above the waves north from the harbour, then, past Ackergill Tower, choose between slow progress over stones at the top of the beach or rough dunes by the edge of the golf-course. I found a narrow path along the crest of the dune before sliding down the sand to where the beach reappeared. Should be easy now... But I'd forgotten that the River Wester at the halfway point is tidal, and the tide was now very high. Every dog-walker in the area knows there is then no way across without a big detour upstream to the road-bridge, I waded in where it looked a bit shallower and ended up wet for the second time that morning, chest-deep in the cold water – remember there had been a frost the previous night – before floundering out on the far bank. The jog back to Keiss just kept me from hypothermia as the water slowly drained from my sodden jogging pants and sweatshirt, the 'easy' run had taken nearly twice as long as planned. It was a good thing I always leave some dry clothes in the car.

Now for a more challenging trip. John O' Groats had been bustling early, a party of a dozen cyclists lining up to

The Stacks of Duncansby

be photographed, tourists pouring onto the Orkney ferry, caravans and camper vans. Shortly after the ferry left I too set off from the harbour for a paddle round daunting Duncansby Head. There was plenty of time before slack water so I stopped on the shell beach for a bite to eat and to pluck up courage for the big headland. I needn't have worried, the sea was almost flat, conditions much more benign than I'd seen off Holburn Head a couple of days earlier. As I pottered round towards the lighthouse, exploring the big geos and caves, it was hard to believe that some of the most ferocious tide-races and seas in the Pentland Firth can be found here.

Several spectacular geos cut into the headland, strikingly seen as you walk the path from the carpark to the stacks, these are even more imposing when explored from the sea, with black overhanging walls under which you paddle. Huge, long caves, unsuspected from above, penetrate Duncansby Head, just wide enough to take a kayak. Cathedral-like incipient geos, with a roof at least 120 feet above the sea, these are perhaps the most impressive on the whole Caithness coast. The Geo of Sclaites – the big geo with a sea-arch at the end – has caves continuing right under the tourist vantage point, with the mooing of seals echoing from the black depths – a thorough exploration to be left for another time, with company!

The cliffs were now largely bare of birdlife, the young guillemots, razorbills and kittiwakes fledged and flying or swimming to their autumn feeding grounds. Only one or two late kittiwakes still sat on untidy nests, while shags, young and old, lined slabby rock ledges. A fierce tide-race normally surges past the most northerly stack at

Grey seals at Duncansby

Paddling Duncansby Head

The main passage into Wifie Geo

Bucholie Castle

Freswick Castle

through the headland into Wifie Geo, one a high, wide passage which could take a small boat, the others narrow slots just wide enough for kayaks and the longest a dark tunnel of well over 100 yards. Having traversed all three, a fourth channel led back to the open sea. A truly amazing place. Look up in any of the high sea caves and you'll see a flat roof composed of reddish sandstone slabs, with obvious fractures and fissures where rocks have fallen into the sea; look down through the clear water and you'll see the boulders on the sea bed. Most probably the rocks won't fall while you are there, but your kayaking helmet would not be much use if they did. The occasional frightening splash is a cormorant or shag, disturbed from a rock ledge and diving, gannet-like, into the water.

More caves at Skirza Head, again with seals mooing from hidden depths, then across the bay to paddle under the windows of Freswick Castle and back along the Freswick sands before landing at Skirza. Paddling alone has its pros and cons, but one of the great advantages is that there is no need for

and almost still. Seals lurched and splashed into the water, three other kayakers appeared from the south, making a morning's trip from Skirza.

Few days give such calm seas, ideal for paddling round the stacks and pottering on down the coast below the red cliffs where all the boulder beaches are crowded with grey seals and their pups in the autumn. Three caves pass

the Knee but with the east-going tide having just faded the waters were calm

Auckengill

to the rarely visited Loch of Lomashion with its resident red-throated diver and chickweed wintergreen on the banks, arctic skuas called from nearby. I stripped off for a quick, refreshing swim to wash off the sweat and salt, it's a good loch for a dip, quite shallow with a gravelly floor.

The croft of Biel of Duncansby is just half a mile away, peat had been cut and laid out to dry in the traditional manner on the moor above. An utterly peaceful spot in the heart of the moors yet just two miles from the bustle of John O' Groats where the car parks were full and tourists were again queueing for photographs at the famous signpost.

I'd now paddled virtually all of the coast between Helmsdale and Tongue. A few days earlier I completed my other tricky headland, St John's Point, an easier proposition provided it is tackled at slack water when the Merry Men of Mey are not dancing. I'd set out from Brough on a warm, calm day, easy paddling except that I was soon too hot.

I've still to get the clothing issue right. Wearing a spray-deck and

those awful, complicated, time-consuming car-shuttles. All I had to do was change into T-shirt and running shoes and set off for a pleasant jog back over the moors to John O' Groats, good to stretch the legs after hours cramped in a little boat. First up the old peat road from Skirza across Black Hill, ending at neglected and abandoned peat workings – in spite of the recession, peat-cutting is too laborious for most folk these days. After just a few hours at sea the sights and scents of land were all the more appreciated, the meadowsweet and blue harebells, the cut grass drying in a field, the heather and peat. Under grey, dappled skies with streaks of blue and gleams of sun, coasts and islands stood out sharp amid glittering seas. Rough, wet moorland led

Scotland's Haven and Stroma

St John's Point

Sunset at Harrow

Sunset from Dunnet Head

buoyancy aid you can't just start stripping off. Yet you need gear that will keep you warm if you end up in the sea, which is very cold at these latitudes. A warm surfing wet-suit is fine for short distances and practicing if you're going to be wet all the time but is too restricting over any distance, a drysuit is usually too hot. I tend to compromise with a 'semi-dry' suit but this would not be warm enough if in the water for a long time, unless wearing lots underneath and is then too hot for prolonged paddling. My best solution is to err on the side of safety and wear too much, then cool off ever so often with a roll or two in some safe shallow location, such as off the little stony beaches below Scarfskerry.

Tides can be quite strong off Scarfskerry Point and Tang Head, I'd timed it so that the main east-going tide was slackening but eddies meant a gentle current against me round to Harrow Harbour. On past the Castle of Mey and Long Geo Farm, to where low broken cliffs run out to St John's Point, again remarkably innocuous in these conditions. Picking my way between the skerries and the mainland I was soon round, a quick dash to Stroma looked tempting but it was choppier now with an east wind and there probably wasn't time before the strong west-going tide picked up. Anyway my energy was lacking for some reason, likely related to age. So, as planned, on past the old harbour at the Bught and along below the overgrown cliffs into the superb bay of Scotland's Haven to land on the beach and watch the curious seals in the water. Then head back the way I'd come, now helped round the Point by the tide.

Rather than paddle all the way back to Brough I'd planned to land at Harrow and jog back to pick up the car. Why was I feeling so sleepy? As I climbed the road from the little harbour I realised it had turned into one

Stormy weather on Dunnet Head

On the western cliffs of Dunnet Head

ampion near the Dunnet Head lighthouse

This stunted aspen, growing on clifftops on the eastern side of Dunnet Head, is possibly the most northerly native tree on the British mainland.

Peedie Bay

of those warm, enervating early afternoons.

The sun, which had remained mostly hidden earlier, beat down. By Scarfskerry I was looking longingly at the cool sea, wishing I'd continued with a gentle paddle and a few rolls and swims! Those five miles back to Brough felt more like the last five of a marathon. Shortcuts look tempting but most tracks end in tall barley and a slow struggle along rough field edges deeply overgrown with long grass, nettles and cleavers. Best stick to the hot tarmac.

Good training perhaps...

Dunnet Head is normally a daunting paddle, but on a sunny summer day of neap tides the main hazard was heat-stroke. I chose to make the journey anticlockwise, from Brough to Dunnet and against the tide, so that I could easily turn back if conditions, with an east wind, proved too boisterous. But I needn't have worried, even if I couldn't linger under the bird cliffs below the lighthouse in the strengthening east-going tide. To be able to make such a trip on an ordinary

Saturday afternoon is little short of miraculous, under those towering cliffs with a cacophony of calls from the colonies of guillemots and kittiwakes, past skerries covered in seals, with

Scots Primrose, Globe Buttercup and Purple Orchid on Dunnet Links. Sadly, in 2012, most were eaten by sheep put to graze too early, in June.

puffins and tysties on the water and an otter diving ahead of me. On, past those great geos I've walked round so often, Red Geo, Ashy Geo, landing on low rocks below the cliffs, waving to sunbathers on the Peedie sands and to folk fishing from a little boat, beaching in

the hot sun on Dunnet Sands. After jogging back to the car through the heat, a delightful swim in the sea at Brough rounded off the afternoon.

If I need to take the car into Thurso and have an hour or two to spare, I'll often go out to Scrabster and jog round the Holburn Head circuit from the Scrabster Hall. The route follows the track up the hill, passing the 'Polo Mint' sculpture to the left and a cottage immediately to the right. After a locked gate the track carries on across the

41

Christmas Day, Dunnet Bay

Scrabster Beach

Thurso East

On Thursdays in summer the Thurso-based Pentland Canoe Club enjoys evening paddles.

moor, you fork left before the old quarries and continue all the way to the trig point on top of Brims Hill.

The track is always exhilarating to follow, so close to the town but already that freedom of the Highlands, high up with views of sky and sea and hill and loch, from Brims Hill you look to the mountains of Sutherland and across the sea to the rolling hills of Hoy. I'd better not mention certain ugly new additions to the landscape to the west and south.

The Deil's Brig, Holburn Head

Head north from the top of the hill to the old stone workings where huge bare slabs of rock remain from the excavations which extended right to the edge of the cliffs, leaving just a narrow lip. It is then simply a case of keeping above the cliffs all the way back round Holburn Head to Scrabster, a distance of some three miles. Some care is needed as just east of the quarry is a huge semicircular bite in the line of cliffs, with an enormous overhanging back wall above a usually boiling sea. It's an ugly place, and to squeeze round the end of a fence takes you uncomfortably near the edge. Mountain-bike tracks indicate that people ride this circuit, I hope they dismount here...

The rest of the route is just a fine jog, enjoying the views of sea and sky, the birds calling and in spring the scents of thrift and squill, with the occasional Scottish primrose to look out for in short turf. In gales you risk being soaked by backwards-blowing waterfalls. Admire the Clett rock, with its colony of black-backed gulls. Discover again the 'Deils Brig', explore (with care) the blowholes and the natural bridge, rest on

the fine stone memorial seat admiring the views of Orkney. The path back to Scrabster has been improved with concrete sleepers bridging the wet patches and with better stiles. I like to take the route along the top of the steep slopes above Scrabster where there are superb views down to the bustling harbour, but if you go down to the lighthouse and through the port there is always the inviting Fishermens' Mission for a cup of tea before climbing the long flight of steps leading back to Scrabster village.

Just rarely in the Far North you get the kind of heat and humidity more normally seen hundreds of miles to the south. We'd been out to Strathy and Armadale on such a day, on the very coast a cool sea-breeze kept the heat at bay, it was one of those days for swimming in the sea and enjoying the fine displays of wildflowers.

In such hot, calm sunny conditions Strathy beach equals or surpasses any in the world. On the machair above the dunes were big patches of purple thyme, white grass of parnassus, yellow kidney vetch with its attendant blue butterflies,

Clett Rock, Holburn Head

The north coast between Melvich and Reay

Lady Bighouse

blue and white milkwort... but not as much as there used to be, there are too many rabbits at Strathy! One only had to walk a little way inland and the heat hit, the temperature in the low eighties, with big white clouds building to the west and south.

It was looking black to the west as I drove down to Thurso in the early evening for the club kayaking session, cars coming through the town had their headlights on. The plan had been to kayak across to Scrabster then take a trip on the Canadian 'Spirit Dancer' 18-seater canoe. I foolishly suggested that the storm would just miss us, but wiser heads prevailed and we took the cars to Scrabster, meeting up at the yacht club. Just as I left the car to walk the few yards to the building a great bolt of lightning hit the top of the cliff in front of me with a simultaneous clap of thunder. Soon rain was lashing down driven by gusty winds, it would have been interesting to say the least to be out in the bay in a little kayak. The Canadian owner of the 'Spirit Dancer' was doing a short presentation in the yacht club, as lightning flashed around, thunder rolled and hail hammered on the windows he was completely at home. 'In some parts of British Columbia we get 400 inches of rain in a year!'

The storm was clearing fast, we'd still be able to go out for a paddle. Smoke though was blowing across, a house on top of the cliffs had been struck and the fire brigade was in attendance, later, out in the bay, we could see the flames. Eighteen of us paddled the 42-foot boat out of

Rough seas off Sandside Head

Corn Sowthistle at Bighouse

Scrabster harbour, my first experience of canoe paddling and the need to keep in sync with 17 others! It was now a lovely evening, waterfalls were pouring off Holburn Head and the boat made light work of the trip round the headland to the Clett Rock. For some reason I'd left my camera behind... and missed the best opportunity I've ever had to photograph that amazing illusion, generated by sloping rock strata, of paddling steeply downhill as you pass through the channel between the Clett and the main cliff. In a kayak it's always too rough to take my hands off the paddle. We paddled back in dazzling warm sunshine, the earlier tantrums now a distant dark cloud over Orkney.

According to good information (well, Google and the internet), the longest sea cave in Britain and the tenth longest in the world is 'cave number two' of Sandside Head, at 230 metres. Yes, a wonder of the world which nobody has ever heard of is right on our doorstep. An adjacent cave, number one, ranks 33rd at 150 metres. And yet. Has anybody actually been there and explored recently? Sometimes tall stories from the distant past get repeated so often they receive the status of fact.

The clifftops between Sandside Bay and Melvich have always been a favourite walk of mine, more folk are doing it now the Caithness Rangers occasionally lead outings there. Not as forbidding as some of the Caithness coast, there are nevertheless spectacular views of sea-stacks and deep rocky bays with the highlight being the largest puffin colony in the north.

The walk only takes two or three hours, or half a day if you take your time. The problem is getting back to the start, I've jogged back along the road or made a day of it with a big circuit inland

Sea-kayaking off Strathy Point

A bay near Portskerra

including Beinn Ratha. This time, for a change, on a July day, I decided to kayak along the foot of the cliffs to Melvich, then enjoy a leisurely stroll back to Reay.

A force four wind from the south was forecast, but the cliffs should give plenty of shelter bar the odd downdraft. I set off early from Sandside Bay, the tide very low with a slight following tide then slack water for rounding the headland to Melvich. Maybe I'd carry on to Strathy, but a weak weather front would be crossing later and the wind could pick up further. The forecast sea

conditions – slight – meant a swell of up to one metre and that is exactly what is was. So sadly, instead of the hoped-for calm sea, there was too much breaking surf to get close to the cliffs or look at those caves.

I hereby lay down a challenge. Which of the Thurso-based Pentland Canoe Club or the Wick-based Caithness Kayak Club will be the first to carry out a definitive exploration of the caves and discover where and how long they are (take a very big ball of string!) And please let me know when you are

going to look. Calm days with no swell are at a premium!

Avoiding the surf, I paddled out round Sandside Head and headed west below rock faces lit by early sun. Even without being able to get in close, the fine rocky coast of cliffs and skerries and stacks – some riddled with caves and passages – could be enjoyed, sparse colonies of kittiwakes and guillemots still called from their ledges, and tysties, black-and-white birds with brilliant red legs, swum in the water.

Ahead was a brief blizzard of several hundred smaller birds coming off one of the stacks – puffins! Suddenly there were dozens on the sea, others looking down from another stack a few hundred yards short of their main

Melvich Beach

breeding site. The swell precluded paddling into the deep geo guarded by the stack, instead I paddled as close as possible on the seaward side, there would be plenty of opportunity to have a good look later from the land.

The wind was indeed picking up as the sky clouded over, sudden downdrafts flattened the sea and grabbed fiercely at the paddle. A pity the weather did not allow for a proper exploration of this spectacular coast, instead the wise thing was to make straight for Melvich harbour then have a more leisurely paddle back along the beach and a short way up the river.

An hour or so later, with the boat out of the water by banks of yellow corn sowthistle near Bighouse, I could look forward to a stroll back along the clifftops with no worries about weather or swell or tide. Conditions were excellent for the walk, a strong wind to keep all the clegs and flies away, warm sun and broken cloud. Not another soul was about. Faint paths, made more by the four-footed than the two-footed, lead most of the way along, sometimes these head down and contour across steep grass above vertiginous drops – remember that sheep have no imagination! The better your head for heights, the more you will see. Right on the county border is a deep, bouldery bay, the entrance a narrow channel, a high sea-stack rising beyond topped with conical slopes in which puffins have made hundreds of burrows. With binoculars you can get a good look from the top of the cliffs, if you are a very experienced scrambler you can make your way down a steep narrow ridge to a grassy promontory right opposite the stack and enjoy the sight of the birds flying to and fro around your head, the waves meanwhile breaking on the stones 100 feet directly below.

I scrambled down to the shore – for the experienced only – where somebody

Oystercatchers on Strathy Beach

A stormy day on Strathy Point

had obligingly constructed two little stone armchairs on which it was possible to comfortably sit, looking straight out through the geo I'd seen from the sea a couple of hours earlier. Do not be tempted to swim or let a dog enter the water, there is a very strong rip tide which will carry anything or anyone out to sea. An increasingly familiar clifftop walk (from Dounreay days!) led eastwards, via the old packhorse bridge and the Scottish Primrose slopes of Sandside Head, to the car at the harbour – just as a sudden downpour of rain and hail lashed across with gusty winds and a rumble of thunder.

Strathy Point is a headland I don't visit often enough given the tremendous cliff scenery. So on a stormy but bright February morning, I jogged along Strathy beach then splashed through the cold River Strathy to gain the steep slopes of the eastern side of the point. Only the determined will stick to the clifftops here, there are many obstacles in the form of fences and deep geos but the rewards lie in seeing small rocky harbours with winches, hidden rock stacks and deep sheltered burn gullies crowded with yellow primroses. Hungry sheep followed, there are less with the new subsidy system and some of the clifftops are reverting to a more natural rough mixture of tussock and heather. Peat is still cut and stacked on Strathy Point, now out of choice rather than necessity, the crofts and houses are modern and well-kept and most of the poverty has thankfully gone.

The old lighthouse buildings had a dilapidated look with peeling white paint and garages open to the elements. The wall gave some shelter from the bitter north-westerly gale for a bite to eat, before continuing my jog along the western side of the point. With high, twisted cliffs, deep geos, rock stacks, natural arches and small rocky islands the scenery here is as fine as any on the north coast and it is well worth carrying on all the way to Armadale Bay – it will take you a whole day to do it justice. Even though I was jogging, there was only time to go as far as the point north of Aultivullin, with a fine view back to the lighthouse above boiling white seas. Easy slopes then led south to a cairn above the two rival B&B's at the end of the Aultivullin road, both in a remote moorland setting with every variety of coastal scenery and wildlife on their very doorstep. Just a little further along the coast is the fascinating Boursa Bay and Island, beyond are blowholes and more bays and eventually the Armadale sands.

With the wind behind me I enjoyed jogging back along the road and down to Strathy village, a nice community, a fine mix of old and new. The riverside path led back to the beach, the tide was now well out and the caves at the far end of the sands open for exploration.

Wifie Geo

Chapter 3   Mountains of Caithness and Sutherland

Foinaven from the east

Summer on Foinaven

Strath Dionard and Spionnaidh from Foinaven

This has been the hardest chapter to write. There is so much wonderful, unvisited mountain country in Sutherland and Caithness. Where to begin! I've made so many expeditions, taken thousands of pictures.... all I can do is give a flavour of these rugged landscapes with a small selection of photos and an account of two or three trips.

The question is frequently asked when I give slideshows of the clifftops and mountains or of kayaking the coast – Do you go alone? The answer, yes, almost always. The next question – do you tell anyone where you are going? Well, usually not!

Ever since climbing my first mountain on my own (in Wales) at the age of 14, I've rarely gone out on the hills with anyone else. I enjoy social walks pottering around the countryside at low levels but the freedom of the hills is mostly lost when in company. Instead of an opportunity to watch the scenery and wildlife and weather, to meditate and think, most of the time is spent talking, or looking out for the safety and comfort of the others.

Frankly, I'm safer on my own. The few times I've got into really unpleasant situations have been when I've gone with companions, supposedly experienced, who have led me into places and dangers of which, on my own, I'd have kept well clear. It's the groups of four – once cited as the minimum number to safely walk the mountains – that get into trouble. On my own, I make sure to keep well within my capabilities. Farmers, crofters, fishermen, creel-boaters go out alone

Our local 'Half Dome' – Silver Rock, Golspie

Watch Hill, Coldbackie

Definitely not Caithness. A tricky section of the Cuillin Ridge.

without telling anyone and nobody worries.

At the age of 19 I spent five weeks walking through the remotest parts of Scotland, up to Cape Wrath, back through the Cairngorms, and no-one knew where I was going. Often I've disappeared into the hills on my own for a few days or a week, without any mobile phone or suchlike. All the Munros were climbed alone, with the exception of the Inaccessible Pinnacle of Skye where I needed a guide to take me up the rock climb to the summit. On my own I swam, without a wetsuit, in every loch in Caithness, and continue to happily swim in out-of-the-way lochs and rivers. I've spent countless nights alone camping or in bothies, with no modern communication gadgets. In the hills, or on uninhabited islands, you don't get lonely. That only happens in towns and cities. The Cuillin ridge is the one place where I'm happier with company, I completed that ridge on my nerves, having to find for myself the way round all the difficult obstacles and traps. A day out with a guide on the classic circuit of Coire Lagan, was the only time I've been really relaxed on the Cuillin and fully able to enjoy the tremendous scenery.

Skye is the exception and rock-climbing is one activity I would not do

The rare Holly Fern growing on Smean

Cloudberry on the slopes of Morven

Morven from Wag, in the Berriedale Glen.

on my own (I'd add to that paddling rivers of more than grade two.) In virtually all of Scotland you can safely walk and scramble in solitude. People who object to my going alone are usually rather envious, they would love to have the freedom of kayaking a gentle river or a wild stretch of coast or walking for miles over the tops without meeting anyone all day, but haven't the courage to attempt it. Indeed, if you lack the confidence to go out alone, don't. However if you go with others don't rely on their ability to rescue you and make sure you have the experience to cope if everybody else gets into difficulties!

On my own I can get an early start. Most folk like to take their time in the mornings, hillwalkers rarely set off before ten while paddling groups are lucky to be on the water by eleven. Much of the day has already gone! If I could be in the office for work by eight,

Scaraben

Maiden Pap

Looking west from Scaraben

East from Scaraben

The view westward from Morven

Morven seen from Small Mount

A long track leads to Braemor from Glutt Lodge

I reckon I should be setting out on the hills or the sea by then, with the whole day ahead without time constraints. OK, in winter maybe 8.30 as it's still dark!

The freedom of having a range of mountains to yourself, or of being able to paddle at your own pace, to land on and explore any little rocky beach, to perhaps just sit for ten minutes watching the waves and listening to the sea-birds, these are things you can only get on your own.

On a superb day early in the year I took the mountain bike and set off (it was after eight, but only just!) up the long estate road through the fine Berriedale woods and out along the Langwell valley to Wag. The track was hard frozen, the wind light, the cycling good. You rarely set out in the Highlands without everyone seeing you and knowing where you are going and I soon met the gamekeeper and told him my plan of heading for Morven then carrying on over the ridge to the west.

From Wag a quad-bike motorway churns through the morass on up the glen, frozen hard it gave excellent walking. Before long I was on the top of Morven, enjoying blue sky, a light dusting of snow and long views over the Caithness and Sutherland landscape with the low winter sun throwing hill shadows far across the sunlit flow country.

Carefully scrambling down the icy boulders, I crossed the usually soggy col to Small Mount, finding easy walking along the frozen peat-hags. Very few people head further west, these are some of the remotest hills in Caithness

and give a fine walk over gravelly, wind-blasted ridges towards Cnoc an Eireannach. All around the empty landscape, nobody about for miles. On Wagmore Rigg the breeze dropped away and I sat for a minute or two in the sun listening to the sound of complete and utter silence.

The old wheelhouse and clearance ruins at Wag basked in enormous quietude, the low sun of early February dipping below the hills, those who once lived here would have made the most of

this fine day for outdoor work, knowing all too well there was plenty of winter still to come. The sun had softened the track surface a little and yellow mud liberally sprayed the bike as I coasted back down the miles to Berriedale, having seen nobody all day until meeting the keeper escaping for the last of the daylight up the glen, having had to spend the day indoors.

Ben Loyal looks like a huge armchair when seen from the Moin road, with the summit An Caisteal as

Looking south-west from Morven across the emptiness of Sutherland towards Ben Klibreck

Ben Loyal from the Kyle of Tongue

Ben Loyal from Tongue

Ben Loyal from Cunside

Roadside sunset

Looking north from Ben Loyal to Tongue and the Causeway

Loch Fhionnaich and Sgor a' Chleirich

Looking east over Loch Loyal to the Griams

the backrest and the ridges of Sgor a' Chleirich and Sgor a' Bhatain as the two arms. It's easy to imagine a mile-tall giant sitting comfortably with his feet on the moor below and his head high above the summit! Two other tops, Sgor Fhionnaich and Sgor Chaonasaid, complete the familiar five-peaked skyline when viewed from the west, the most dramatic aspects of the peak are seen if you climb from this side. Lovely birch woods here cover the steep lower slopes and those who don't fancy climbing can enjoy a good walk along the foot of the mountain to Loch an Dherue. East of the main massif are two more worthwhile hills, Ben Hiel and Cnoc nan Cuilean, both steep, rough, and rarely climbed. From Skerray the latter top shows up as a sharp

triangle like a miniature Schiehallion.

For all the drama when seen from below, the main ridge is a gentle walk over wide rounded slopes of moss and very short heather, with just an easy scramble to reach the highest point. A challenge is to visit all the ten tops of the peak in one day. Somehow it always seems to happen after a long walk over

this pathless, rough mountain country that at least one of those outlying peaks, which all require big descents and re-ascents, gets omitted. So I would make a determined attempt, lightly clad with running shoes and a very small rucksac, have an early start, and follow a carefully planned route which would first cross two of the most awkward tops. The forecast was good, though with rising wind and a possibility of rain late.

Early traffic was heading for Dounreay as I drove west, to leave the car shortly after eight at Lettermore, halfway along Loch Loyal. I jogged southwards, turning off the road just before Loch Loyal Lodge to begin climbing the rocky slopes leading onto Cnoc nan Cuilean. There are some delightful hill lochans on the shoulder of this peak, and the less-energetic walker could have a good day just exploring this hill. The views from the summit over the vast expanses of Sutherland moor and mountain are nearly as good as those from Ben Loyal itself.

The route from this, the easternmost of the outlying peaks, to the westernmost, is the most awkward part of the traverse. First a big descent to Loch Nam Beist, then a contouring climb round the lower slopes of Ben Loyal proper, to reach a subsidiary top of An Creagan. Quad bike tracks leading up from the valley help, this is how motorised stalkers gain the main Ben Loyal ridge. The sharp peak of Sgor Fhionnaich, above Loch Fhionnaich

then comes into view, but there is still an awkward half-mile of steep broken slopes to cross.

The long narrow Loch Fhionnaich, between the vertical crags of Sgor a' Chleirich and the tumbled house-size boulders of Sgor Fhionnaich, is one of the finest secrets of Ben Loyal, the sheer rock face above would be a famous climbing ground anywhere else.

Loch Fhionnaich from Sgor a' Chleirich

These two peaks are quite tricky, with traps for the unwary, and most easily climbed in the direction I was taking. Sgor Fhionnaich is straightforward from the south end of the loch but the only easy route onward is then to retreat the same way and climb up to the south of those tremendous crags on Sgor a' Chleirich. A much more spectacular route though is to make a very steep descent, a 60 degree slope of grass and heather, straight from the summit. This leads into a maze of huge boulders piled on the slope unlike anything I know anywhere else. Many of these are the size of houses, with caves underneath which could shelter a small army, or any number of illicit whisky stills. Pick your way down carefully, there are hidden drops into deep holes! A narrow sandy beach at the north end of Loch Fhionnaich, under beetling cliffs, is another of my favourite spots, then follows an awkward climb between the crags with one scramble I never really like up a little gully. Once past this bad step, easy but steep grass leads to Sgor a' Chleirich and on a fine day you are back on top of the world, perched high above the loch with the valley way, way below.

The main difficulties were now over, but the wind had risen to a bitterly cold near gale from the south. I had to detour into that wind to pick up the fourth summit, the rounded and gravelly Carn an Tionail, then head back north above long cornices of old snow to the next mossy top of Beinn Bheag. These smooth, Grampian-like tops are a complete contrast to those 'Sgors' seen from the west.

Now, just along the ridge, was the highest rocky tor of An Caisteal which needs some easy scrambling to reach the very top, care was needed on the summit in the gusty wind with vertical crags immediately below. North and west are the two remaining high points on the main ridge, both spectacular viewpoints and well worth visiting even if you don't manage any of the other ten

An Caisteal

The summit of Ben Loyal

West from Sgor a' Bhatain

Evening light, Sgor a' Chaonasaid

tops. Sgor a' Bhatain has a rocky tor – awkward to climb in the gale – and a lower top which directly overlooks the Kyle of Tongue, both are prominently seen in views of the mountain from the west. Next I contoured round bouldery slopes to regain the main ridge and the final tops of Sgor a' Chaonasaid. The wind was too strong to attempt the various rock tors here, but with care I could scramble onto the highest point. Here too is what I call 'The old man of Ben Loyal', a remarkable natural face in the rock. These northernmost tops

have a tremendous view, almost overhanging the Kyle of Tongue, seemingly thousands of feet below.

Two more summits remained. The rock slabs and boulders of Creag Riabhach, blasted now by the southerly gale, were just a short ascent above a similarly-named lochan. The last isolated top of Ben Hiel required a big descent to a boggy col followed by a 750-foot climb. The direct route down to the col is very steep with broken crags, it is much better to head northwards first. Long easy slopes then led at last, to this

The Old Man of Ben Loyal

tenth top. Although late April, the hills were still very wintry without much life other than for herds of deer and a greenshank calling near Loch na Beiste, but on my way back over the lower

Ben Hope from Ben Loyal

slopes I came across a little wooded ravine, sheltered from the wind. Here chaffinches, blue tits and robins were singing in the bare trees while primroses gave a splash of Spring yellow among the dead bracken.

The circuit of the tops had taken me just seven hours by dint of jogging most of the level and downhill stretches, and I drove back east to meet the last of the traffic heading homeward from Dounreay.

The Assynt landscape of isolated peaks is one of the most striking and beautiful in the Highlands, if not the world. Although on the clearest of days the top of Ben More Assynt is visible from near my home, the area is not easy

Heading for the Griams – the old forest road over Slettil Hill

Dawn over Loch Eileanach and Ben Griam Beg

Ben Griam Mor from Ben Griam Beg

Looking towards the Knockfins from Ben Griam Beg

Ben Klibreck from Meall a' Bhata, above Loch Choire

Ben Klibreck from Loch Choire

Loch Badanloch

Towards the Griams from Ben Armine

Loch Naver from Ben Klibreck

A young fawn on the slopes of Ben Hope

Ptarmigan on Ben Hope

This young hare was hiding under a rock on Ben Hope

The eastern slopes of Ben Hope

Loch Hope from Ben Hope

Looking down the steep west face of Ben Hope

South-west from Ben Hope

Sunset over Ben Loyal and Ben Hope

to reach by public transport. Consequently my visits have been either on those rare occasions when the car is available or else when making a long trek across the far north-west on foot. I first crossed that wild part of Sutherland some 40 years ago, sleeping out one

Quinag

Views from Quinag

night on the very summit of Suilven, watching fog spread in below from the sea till my peak was an island above it. Twice, with a full camping pack, I've struggled over the precipitous Bealach Chornaidh on Quinag between Kylesku

North-east from Quinag

North from Quinag

Quinag

and Loch Assynt. The first such occasion was not planned, I was making a fortnight's trek from Lochcarron to Cape Wrath too late in the season, with day after day of low cloud and rain. I'd meant to follow the glens to the east of Ben More but was turned back by deer stalking and had to detour by Suilven and Quinag instead. So these two mountains are always linked in my mind.

A brief two-day interlude of clear, crisp weather in mid-November, with the car available, gave an overdue opportunity for a return visit to Quinag

and Suilven. Before seven I was driving south over slushy roads, the first snow of the winter on the Ord. By 9-30 the car was parked below Quinag, north of Inchnadamph, a powdering of snow on the ground, the snow-dusted peaks above crisp in early sunshine.

Another man was setting off, he looked like a mountain guide or fitness instructor on his day off and disappeared ahead up the hill with a long stride at a cracking pace. Quinag is a roughly 'Y'-shaped mountain, with high peaks at all the extremities and a

steep, undulating ridge between them. It's a superb expedition to tackle all the tops, but you need to be fairly fit to enjoy it as there are many big descents and re-ascents. I would have to be quite fast, intending also to walk out to Suilven in the late afternoon. A wet and eroded path led easily up to a great corrie and a loch below three of the main peaks, then a steep but easy climb took me to the ridge leading to the highest top. A couple of inches of soft snow gave added beauty to the views without making the walking difficult or

dangerous and for the next few hours I trod the airy ridges, from the northernmost top to the southernmost, taking my time on the many steep climbs to enjoy the tremendous scenes. The air was almost calm with patchy, dappled cloud, and with light snow showers enveloping the Foinaven range to the north. Lochs Glencoul and Glendhu, beyond the Kylesku Bridge, were mirror-calm. Below Quinag's high craggy western ramparts the low sunlight illuminated the loch-and-cnocan landscape towards Drumbeg, the rocky knolls glowing red above dark shadowed hollows and lochs. The other isolated Assynt peaks marched south – Suilven, Canisp, Culmor, beyond were the rugged mountains south of Ullapool, then the Torridon hills and even, hazily in the distance, the Cuillin of Skye some 80 miles away. Westward, across the sea, were the moors of Lewis and the far hills of Harris. All was calm and still, the sun setting as I picked my way down over rock slab and boulder on the south ridge to gain a very wet and eroded path leading back to the car.

A few miles west of Quinag, at the end of Loch Assynt, a path leaves the road and climbs southwards over the knolls to a bothy below Suilven. A little signpost encouragingly says 'Suileag 5 km'. It is well known that Highland miles are long ones, but if this sign is correct, kilometres are even longer.

It was a good thing some daylight remained. An indistinct and very wet path led to a bridge, fortunately still extant, over the swollen River Inver. Here an obvious route carried straight on, leading into very wet boggy ground and petering out. Somehow I'd missed the way. Continuing westward, sloshing through bogs and a river in fading light, I found the path again which became a very rough, wet and mostly narrow trod, climbing up through a notch in the hills. I stopped to empty the water out of my boots but needn't have bothered, the path wasn't a good one to follow in the dark, very boggy and with hidden holes where I twice went in up to the thigh. The last of the sunset glow faded from Quinag with the western isles still darkly outlined against a red sky, a hard frost was setting in. Snow-dusted Suilven,

The Suilven Ridge, looking west

Suilven

now illuminated by moonlight, rose straight ahead. But the route was clear and by torchlight and the light of the moon steady progress was made past lochan and over cnocan until a whiff of coal-smoke told me that the bothy was near. A group of five lads from an Ambleside college course on 'Outdoor Studies' was already in residence with a roaring fire of coal they'd carried in from Lochinver. Great to take off soaking socks and boots, and warm up by the fireside with a mug of tea.

To have time to walk back out by daylight meant an early start the next morning for Suilven, a mountain which looks impregnable but is quite easy if you gain the ridge at the col between the two main peaks. Being one of the most striking peaks in Scotland, it is a very popular objective and the routes leading onto the ridge are badly eroded. As dawn came up a single red contrail stretched from horizon to horizon in an otherwise totally clear sky, the glen remaining in frozen shadow as the rising sun gleamed red on the broken crags of the mountain. For a couple of miles a good stalkers' path leads up the valley before the walkers' route to Suilven turns south – never having been properly made, this is mostly a morass.

In the permanent winter shadow of the peak the ground continued freezing all day, giving a much easier return walk.

The climb to the ridge was steep but easy, suddenly to emerge into brilliant sunshine and a cold wind on the crest. Views were even clearer than the day before, the Cuillin now sharp on the far horizon, every mountain in Sutherland and Wester Ross cloud-free and basking in the low November sunlight, with Suilven's familiar outline etched out in shadow across the low ground to the north. The ridge to the main peak had a very airy feel to it in lying snow and a gusty wind, a walker's footprints left the day before had frozen into ice giving the odd slippery patch. You sense the surrounding vertical crags below, the only way back down is the way you came! The view from the snowy summit over miles of moor and lochan is a little reminiscent of that from Morven, similarly an isolated peak, but is still more spectacular in its views of the other Assynt peaks and the high mountains to the south. Beyond the white houses of Lochinver, five miles away, was the blue sea with Lewis in the

The Suilven wall

Suileag bothy and Canisp

Suilven from Suileag

far distance, southwards a tiny toy boat was heading out into the Minch past the Summer Isles – the ferry bound from Ullapool to Stornoway.

Carefully I picked my way back to the col and started up the other top to the east. This ridge is narrower and more difficult, and I didn't like the look of the last part of the climb under snow. So I turned back, instead enjoying a more relaxed descent to the glen and a walk down to the bothy, the valley path wandering in and out of Suilven's shadow. On a crisp winter mid-afternoon in the Highlands you can

sometimes find a sheltered spot where the sun is warm and almost kid yourself it's summer. It was like that back at the bothy, sitting out on a sunlit bench with a mug of tea, looking up to the peak I'd just climbed. The sun doesn't linger long though, and neither could I if I didn't want to be caught by darkness. It was however an enjoyable walk out, much easier in daylight with the ground now partly frozen, Quinag ahead catching the last of the sun. The '5 km' took me nearly two hours, the moon was rising, my boots were caked in ice and the car was already frozen by the time I reached

the road at the end of the loch.

A classier approach to Suilven is by kayak, from the east, and this was a trip I made under very different conditions.

After a lifetime of wandering through the wilder parts of the Scottish Highlands, I thought I knew the insect hazards of the summer season pretty well. The author of the Book of Revelation, Chapter 9, could have advised me better...

Even familiar insects can cause considerable grief to the unprepared. Ticks I like least, they fasten on and can

The shadow of Suilven

The rarely climbed easternmost top of Suilven

give you the very unpleasant Lyme's disease if you don't get them off within a day or so. Vegetation more than ankle high swarms with them, the worst are the tiny ones at the beginning of their life cycle which are almost invisible. Next stage is a size up, the freckle that crawls, whilst the adults are half the size of a ladybird with a handsome red mark and a nasty bite. I'm pretty paranoid about them, covering up and constantly checking for the insects on clothing. Even so, after a foray into the great outdoors there are always one or two which have evaded my defences.

There are enough midgie tales to fill several books. Midges are rarely a problem provided you keep moving, except after a big hatch in calm weather, when you may have to run to avoid the swarms. Camping in midges is something of an art, but with a midge-proof inner tent, mosquito coils and a midge hat you can manage. The only repellent that works when midges are seriously bad is DEET – folk who recommend bog myrtle or skin-so-soft or whatever have never met real midgie swarms – and even then the insects will find the little bit of skin that's not covered. Midges are a pest, a nuisance, a serious deterrent to summer, lowland camping but you can usually cope, even if it means sitting sealed inside a tent on a fine summer evening.

Some folk hate clegs. But their season is quite short and they are fairly slow insects, only come out in warm weather, normally attack in just ones or twos and are easily swatted when they land. If they bite, you feel a sharp prick and can flick the insect off before any significant damage is done. I have, though, on rare occasions been attacked by a swarm of a dozen or two when crossing the Caithness moors and one's entire attention is then devoted to fighting the things off.

The main Suilven Ridge, looking east

Looking towards Stac Polly from Cul Mor

One of the worst nuisances is the sweat-sucking fly, slightly larger than a housefly, which can swarm around you in huge black clouds on a hot day, trying to land and drink your sweat. There's little you can do except attempt to wave them off and just keep going till you reach fresher, windier conditions. Then there are the familiar mosquitoes which bite quietly without you knowing anything about it till you notice an itchy lump. Being aware they are around, using repellent, covering up is the best protection. And don't pitch your tent on an ants' nest! It's easier said than done, as the few dry spots in wet Highland ground are the places favoured by these little biters.

August is often the worst month, but at the end of June none of these pests should yet be too bad. My plan was to kayak to the end of Loch Veyatie, in the heart of Assynt west of Elphin, try out a brand new tent for the night, then climb Suilven the next morning before paddling out and heading for home. A track leads from the road for about half a mile down to the loch where there is a salmon hatchery, a locked gate bars vehicles so it was a case of lifting everything over the gate, strapping the kayak to a little two-wheeled trolley and trundling it down the hill. An hour after arriving I was paddling westward up the quiet, grey loch on a damp, muggy, afternoon threatening more rain. The narrow Loch Veyatie stretches for several miles west into the hills, all empty roadless country, with scattered birchwoods along the hilly shores. Under the grey, misty skies the feeling was of entering a truly wild place. The promised rain began, I paddled into a small stony beach below the trees to put on my waterproof top. This took a while, having to remove the life-jacket, and a swarm of little insects gathered, I thought at first they were midges but they were bigger, and more determined.

Dressed in all my gear I was pretty well protected from them, whatever they were, but headed out as quickly as possible into the loch.

Dimly through rain and drifting mist rose the isolated peaks of Culmor and Suilven. I paddled on down the long, narrow loch, stopping again to land briefly on a shingle spit and just savour the peace and solitude of this place. The rocky country south of the loch had been burnt by huge fires in early May, but most of the scattered birches had survived and already the landscape was green with fresh growth.

At the far end of the loch was a rare perfect campsite, a grassy knoll just above the shore and sufficiently breezy, I hoped, to dispel the midges. In the heavy rain I set about erecting my new tent for the first time, it was a modern hooped design and I needed to follow the written instructions. Unfortunately these were printed on flimsy paper which rapidly disintegrated under the downpour and it was a race to get the tent up before they became completely illegible.

A couple of dozen of those pesky little flies had followed me into the tent, some kind of biting black fly I thought and hunted down as many as possible before cooking my tea. Unfortunately the odd one must have been missed which, unknown to me, enjoyed its own meal. The weather relented later, allowing me an evening walk into the very rough country of rocky knolls and lochans below the towering crags of Suilven, on top of one knoll was a tiny lochan not even marked on the map – with a red-throated diver calling its weird wails. I now noticed I'd been bitten – one or two nasty red spots – and did my best to fend of the determined insects back at the tent. By the next day the bites had become huge itchy sores the size of a 50p piece, the worst bites or stings I've ever had.

The classiest way into Suilven

Cul Mor and Cul Beag from Suilven

After visiting both summits I was back at the tent on a lovely sunny late morning with most thankfully a good breeze to keep down the insects. An idyllic, quiet spot but whenever the wind dropped those flies were not far away... nevertheless I could enjoy taking my time packing up, listening to the sandpipers and the curlews and the distant wailing of divers while the scent of thyme rose from the short grass in the sunshine.

The wind helped me back along the loch, a lovely easy paddle to Elphin. I'd received six awful bites in spite of my efforts to fend the insects off, had I been less careful I'd likely have ended up in hospital. Whatever were the things? Birch flies. Supposedly only found on Speyside, but the Assynt folk would hardly advertise that their part of the world has them. Sometimes called 'super-midges', their bite is known to be very nasty, far worse than a mosquito, and folk have indeed ended up needing medical attention. And yet the Highlands would not be the wild and wonderful area it is, without its hazards of insect life in addition to weather and

The morning was bright, fresh and breezy. By 6.30 I was on my way up through that tangled country, soon climbing steeper and steeper slopes to gain the col between the two tops of Suilven. Here the illusion that you've reached somewhere really remote is rudely dispelled in the form of a very fine dry-stone wall built right across the col, huge stones emplaced on a ridiculously steep hillside. Nobody seems to know why this wall was constructed at incredible effort, or by whom. Perhaps it was a scheme to provide employment during the Highland Potato Famine 160 years ago, like a wall built across Ben Dearg to the southwest. A work of art, a truly amazing piece of architecture.

Loch Choire

Rainbow over Strath Dionard

Scaraben footbridge

The shadow of Morven

rough country. There's a place even for
birch flies... as long as its not where I
happen to be!

The Rabbit Isles from Watch Hill

Loch Eribol from Creag na Faolinn

Morven, Smean and Carn Mor from Maiden Pap

Chapter 4   Islands

The Rabbit Isles

The appeal of islands, especially uninhabited islands, is one of those things that grows as you get older. I would love to emulate the man who has slept on all the 162 larger Scottish islands but somehow I don't think it's an ambition I'm likely to achieve.

One of the best ways of visiting an island is by sea-kayak. When you're really experienced (which I most certainly am not) a sea-kayak is one of the most seaworthy boats ever to take to the water, and can happily cope with conditions up to force eight gale – though my limit is force three to four! To build up experience takes time, the best way to learn is to join a local club of which there are two excellent ones in Caithness, the Pentland Canoe Club and the Caithness Kayak Club, which will provide all the equipment you need until you've reached the stage of wanting to buy your own boat.

Spending a night alone on an uninhabited island is not, however, a thing many people have done. After my first season of sea-paddling, the friendly Rabbit Isles, near Tongue, provided a good challenge for a novice kayaker. To

Primroses on the Rabbit Isles

A view to Sgeir an Oir, Rabbit Isles

Sunset over the Kyle of Tongue

Looking across the islands to Ben Hope

A tricky landing on Sgeir an Oir

A view from Sgeir an Oir

paddle the shortest way across from Talmine would be just too easy, instead I'd set off from the old pier opposite the House of Tongue, near the causeway. There would be about three miles to paddle, all quite near the shore and so pretty safe for someone with my basic level of skill. It was, though, October, which meant quite a swell coming into Tongue Bay even though the forecast was for light winds.

Late on a lovely autumn afternoon I unloaded the boat from the car and carried it down to where the old, seaweed-covered slipway entered the water. This manhandling of a heavy boat is perhaps more hazardous than the paddling! I stowed camping gear and food into the watertight compartments, donned wetsuit and buoyancy aid and paddled off into the sunshine and rippling water. Just a gentle swell was coming down the Kyle, the tide was flooding in, which was against me but in the event of any serious mishap I wasn't going to be swept out to sea.

The scent of the sea mingled with that of yellowing autumn leaves as I paddled below wooded slopes, behind me Ben Hope and Ben Loyal basked in early evening sunshine. Ahead, a line of breakers warned that things were not going to stay quite so placid. Where the open sea of Tongue Bay meets the more

Orkney – an empty beach on the Isle of Sanday

A lonely Orkney isle – sea kayaking lets you visit places like this.

On Graemsay, Orkney

the rest of the paddle past Ard Skinid, across the choppy channel and round the first island, to beach the kayak on the second isle where the only footprints on the pristine sand were those of an otter.

There was just time for a quick look round the first island before the narrow spit of sand which joins the two was submerged by the rising tide, with breakers coming in from the west. With barely an hour of daylight left I made a quick exploration of the second isle before setting up the tent above the shore as dark fell. Both islands are quite gentle, with a lot of blown sand and marram grass, otherwise rock outcrops and boggy patches and tussocks and thistles. There are rocky shores and some low cliffs and geos, in spite of the

sheltered waters of the Kyle, the swell foams and breaks on various sand bars and spits, earlier I'd spied out the sea from Coldbackie and reckoned that I could avoid the worst. Now the tide had risen further and the area of confused water had moved so as to block my route round the end of the sands below Ard Skinid. The swell was growing bigger and there were breaking waves ahead.

The shore was near and, if I couped it, the waves and current would take me onto the beach in a minute or two.

Otherwise I'd never have tried it on my own. I didn't though want the ignominy of capsizing with, no doubt, half a dozen pairs of binoculars trained upon me from the roads and houses which look across this very visible stretch of water! With waves of up to six feet breaking over me from two directions at once it was the most difficult sea I'd yet been out in... and it was with great relief that after a couple of hundred yards I was through the worst and just had to cope with a big smooth swell. Soon this too subsided and I could relax and enjoy

Eilean nan Ron, loch and sea-arch

The cliffs and moors of west Hoy are one of the wildest and least-visited places in the North. This scenery is near the Candle of the Sneuk.

name I never saw any sign of rabbits. Something, perhaps otters, makes faint trods across the islands, or maybe it was the two wild sheep with long unkempt wool enjoying life having missed years of rounding up and dipping and clipping. A big black segmented beetle became, unknown to me, wrapped up in the tent when I later packed up… and subsequently bit me when I tried to remove it back at home.

Cloud was moving in, settling down over the darkling mountains and obscuring the last of the sunset. A strip of orange lights gleamed incongruously across the bay from Coldbackie. My desert island was hardly remote!

As the tide flowed and ebbed overnight I listened to the changing sound of the sea, just breakers when the spit of sand was submerged, then two different sets of waves washing in as the tide went out, the smaller waves on my side hissing onto the sands. The light wind, only force three when I'd set off, had now as forecast almost completely dropped away.

The morning dawned calm and grey, patches of mist clinging to hillsides above the sea. With the tide high again I paddled back across to the first island, landing to explore properly. A very quiet, peaceful place, save for the remains of two buzzards, quite likely poisoned, by the cairn marking the highest point. Of the two islands, this one seemed more feminine with grassy slopes and even some low scrubby willow, the other masculine with more in the way of cliffs and rocks. Both are delectable spots on a fine summer day.

Evening light on the Old Man of Hoy, seen from the 1200-foot cliffs of St John's Head

relaunch again into the placid waters of the Kyle of Tongue. I know my own limits (or maybe I'm a coward). The hard part of the journey over, I could now enjoy a gentle paddle up the Kyle to the causeway, looking up at the misty hillsides and the autumn colours of moor and tree.

As my sea-kayak experience increased, my island trips became more ambitious. Places that were once completely inaccessible to me now came within easy reach. A kayak and all the equipment is quite expensive – but even just the trips I've had to Eilean nan Ron have been well worth the money spent.

In gently rippling seas and a light breeze I paddled out from the stony beach at Skerray, shortly after eight in the morning. Skies were grey, a weak weather front was approaching and though the forecast was for light winds all day, I was expecting it to pick up briefly around lunchtime when the front came through.

It took barely 20 minutes to reach the cliffs of Eilean nan Ron and the old harbour. There's a little 'inner' harbour

Setting off again, I was soon paddling past Ard Skinid with waves breaking on the rocks. Indeed the swell was a little higher than the day before and, with the tide now on the ebb, the current and the waves would be working against each other. As I paddled along the sandy shore towards the channel leading into the Kyle, the height of the swell picked up. Ahead I could see a mass of confused water and breaking waves, this time the tide would be sweeping me away from the beach. Any red-blooded kayaker would have just charged as the first big foam-topped swell rose ahead... but there is a chicken route. I turned and made for the beach where the swell was a bit less. Then dragged and carried the laden kayak across a quarter of a mile of sand-spit to

Looking across Eilean nan Ron

here, reached by a short sea-cave at low tide, the tide was though nearly up to the roof of the cave so I left a visit until later. Northwards, another fine sea-cave leads through to a sheltered inlet but with too much swell for my liking I gave it a miss. The north-east corner of the island has a huge cave running through the headland but again there was too much swell to attempt it. So, helped by a west-going tide, I paddled on round the spectacular tumbled cliffs and rocks of

The old harbour, Eilean nan Ron

Up from the harbour – take care!

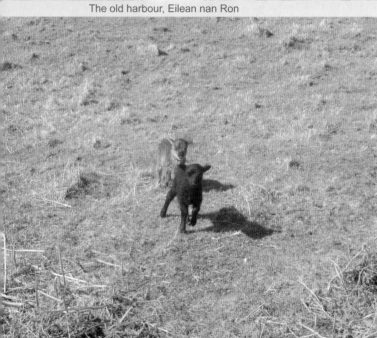

Eilean nan Ron lambs

Looking towards the old schoolhouse

Looking towards Neave Island from Eilean nan Ron

The view towards Ben Hope

Landing beach, Eilean nan Ron

Meall Thalim – a place I've never set foo

Meall Thalim

the north coast of the island to where a narrow channel cuts south dividing the island from the neighbouring Eilean Iosal – a place I'd never visited, and the day's main objective.

There are no good landings on Eilean Iosal. Sheep graze, apparently abandoned, and now live a healthy and wild lifestyle away from shearing and dipping and rounding-up. How were they landed and taken off? I paddled on around the cliffs and deep inlets, taking a narrow channel east of the outer rocks of Meall Thalim. Eventually, on the southern side of the island, I found a little inlet in the barnacle-covered rocks where I could haul the boat out of the water, and set off to explore an island which very few folk have ever visited. Although only a hundred acres or so in size, it must be a couple of mile's walk around the indented coastline, amazing scenery of tumbled rocks and contorted cliffs. The tussocky grass and heather are well-grazed by the wild sheep, perhaps the Soay or North Ronaldsay breed, small, mostly dark animals and tups with big curly horns – indeed it was strange to see a mixed flock with as

On Eilean Iosal

many tups as ewes. Also, one or two little lambs. The sheep seemed fairly tame but I kept my eyes on the tups, not wanting to be suddenly butted from behind when standing on the edge of a cliff.

As expected the wind was picking up, with piled clouds to the west heralding the approaching weak front, it was time to be on my way. So scramble

down to the boat, change back into wetsuit (it all takes time) and launch again, detouring up the narrow channel dividing the two islands to complete the circumnavigation of Eilean Iosal, the screaming of oystercatchers echoing between the cliffs. The tide was now low, with only just enough water for the boat, a great advantage of a plastic kayak is that a few bangs on submerged rocks

Big arch, Eilean nan Ron

The western side of Eilean nan Ron

do it no harm. Some of the sheep had made their way down ledges to the sea and were eating the seaweed, emulating the wild cattle on Swona.

Now southward and across the bay of Port na h-Innse with choppy waves from the side and more 'lumpy' water around the headland. The tide would be just starting to take me eastward as I paddled through the Caol Raineach and on round the southern corner of the island back to the little harbour which now, at low tide, was accessible through the cave. More hazardous is the old,

Sheep of Eilean Iosal

steep flight of steps with broken railings leading upwards.

For a couple of hours I wandered over Eilean Nan Ron as the cloud cleared and the sun came out. The little black and white sheep with tiny new lambs were delightful, but as always the ruined houses were sad. Part of one of them used to be the schoolhouse. The booklet 'The story of Island Roan' by John George Mackay, and available from the Skerray shop, shows a picture of the last two pupils in the school, with the impressive sum £1,678 -19s- 03/4d

This beach on Neave Island is seen in the distance from Bettyhill

Thrift on the western clifftops of Neave Island

multiplied by 674 on the blackboard! Now the old schoolhouse is two feet deep in sheep dung with all the windows and doors out. I crossed the top of the island, with its 360 degree views of ocean and Kyle and mountain, I carefully followed the edges of some of the fearsome cliffs, I admired the deep cleft with its loch and sea-cave, just north of the old village. I walked through the old peat workings on Cnoc na Caillich, noting a dozen or so pairs of bonxies which would soon, when their chicks had hatched, be viciously attacking any intruders.

With wind, waves and tide behind me it only took 15 minutes to paddle back across and land on the stony beach of my third island of the day, Neave. So close to the mainland that you could swim across, it's a wild and wonderful place of tremendous cliffs, huge geos, sea stacks and a lovely sandy beach. Sometime I'll spend the night on this most peaceful of islands and explore at leisure, now I just had a quick walk along the top of the overhanging crags to the summit of the island and looked down into some of the deep chasms to the north. Five minutes of gentle paddling across the sunlit water then took me back to the beach at Skerray, to land on the stones some nine hours after setting out.

Has anybody else ever enjoyed a day which began on Eilean Hoan, north of Durness, took in a circumnavigation of Handa Isle and ended at a remote bothy east of Kylesku at the head of Loch Glencoul? No, I didn't have a fast RIB, just a sea-kayak and a car.

Western cliffs of Neave Island.

The beach of Neave Island

A spectacular view across Graemsay and Orkney from Ward Hill, Hoy

A tropical beach on Handa

Eilean Hoan, looking towards Durness and towards Whiten Head

Late in the afternoon of the previous day I'd driven round the last bend of the twisty Loch Eriboll road to see a huge swell rolling into the sands of SangoBeg. My plan had been to kayak out to Eilean Hoan, just a mile offshore, but no way was I launching through that surf with so many people on the beach to watch my likely capsize!

I never like the touristy atmosphere of Durness but had no option but to park by the visitor centre and try setting out from Sango Bay, where the surf was marginally less. Indeed visitors were down on the beach taking photos of the white breaking rollers, while I, attempting to look the nonchalant experienced mariner, dragged the kayak laden with camping gear into the surf. This spot is overlooked, too, by a big caravan site… fortunately I made it out successfully without being washed back clinging to an upturned boat. It was a couple of miles from here to Eilean Hoan, by no means a gentle paddle with the swell bouncing off the cliffs giving rise to that confused water known as clapotis, and far too rough to paddle in

for a look at Smoo cave.

Forty-five minutes later I thankfully reached the shelter of Hoan with seals and tranquil waters of waving kelp. The RSPB own the island and have a little bothy just above the sandy beach on the southern shore, a lovely spot to spend the night after a late-evening's potter around watching the sun going down, with showers still to the south over the cloud-capped hills of Foinaven. So near the tourist rush but so far removed from it.

The RSPB bothy on Eilean Hoan

hosting large sea-bird colonies.

The bay was sheltered from the open sea by many skerries and small islands, I paddled out from the beach in hot sunshine, rounding various rocky shores before a short crossing to the low cliffs of Handa. It would, I'd assumed, be too rough to paddle round the island but easy to head north then westward along the rising cliffs before turning back. However there was less swell here, and it was quite manageable to carry on, rounding each little headland to find higher and higher cliffs. Colonies of cliff-nesting kittiwakes, guillemots and razorbills there were, but less in numbers than you see on the east coast of Caithness. Here was the great stack of Handa, a huge 400-foot high block with a narrow passage between it and the island with the swell surging through – not to be attempted on my own. On the clifftops, tiny figures of tourists were watching the birds with binoculars. Round another headland, past skerries and through a small tidal overfall then, almost to my surprise, I was approaching the sheltered southern side of the island. A mile on was a

Later that night a local fishing boat, seeing the kayak on the shore, made sure I knew he was there with a rattling engine and loud music, then gave a big toot when coming back at seven the next morning. Oh well. Everyone from Kinlochbervie to Tongue now knew that Ralph had spent the night on Eilean Hoan.

The morning's paddle back to Durness was just as rough as the journey across, with the added excitement of a surf landing on Sango Bay under the eyes of a hundred caravanners. The day was though shaping up for the best of the week, clear and sunny with very light winds. There would be no better opportunity for a paddle to Handa Island, a place I'd never visited. The roads had been quiet, I turned off down to Tarbet – and couldn't believe the dozens of cars parked near the harbour where a little boat was shuttling tourists across to Handa. Owned by the Scottish Wildlife Trust, this small island is roughly circular and about a mile in diameter with 400-foot cliffs on its western side

The western cliffs of Handa

Looking south from Handa

chicks. The famous puffins? Saw none, the Caithness stack at Drumholiston is much better than anything Handa can offer. A gentle paddle through sunlit waters took me back to Tarbet.

I'd have liked to spend the night on an offshore island but didn't trust the forecast, cloud was thickening from the west which usually indicates strengthening south-easterly winds. So instead I drove the few miles to Kyelsku for another trip I'd always wanted to do, up the loch to Glencoul bothy, a place I'd only previously visited by means of a long overland trek from Loch Shin. From the Kylesku Bridge the two arms of the sea loch, Glencoul and Glendhu, stretch tantalisingly into the distance, backed by steep rocky mountains. Few take the opportunity to do other than look.

In the late afternoon sun I packed the boat by the old ferry slipway and set off for the third time that day, into the calm sea-loch. There's no path to the head of Loch Glencoul, on foot it's a rough, arduous trek but by kayak or canoe, just an easy three-mile paddle, coasting along looking at the steep

magnificent sandy beach, totally deserted like a tropical paradise under the hot sun, just the place for a late lunch.

A well-made path, with board-walks, circuits the island with spectacular views of the cliffs and bird colonies, though for the best views you have to defy the warning notices and leave the path. The summit of Handa gave a superb 360 degree view of the rocky west coast and the mountains of Quinag and Assynt to the east and south. I felt a bit guilty in jogging round in under an hour, it would have justified much longer especially on such a fine day, but at least I'd had a flavour of the nature reserve. Skuas nest, this is the only place I've seen an arctic skua attacking a great skua which had come too close to its

Sunlit seas off Handa

rocky shoreline. And so, a day which had begun at a bothy on Eilean Hoan ended at a bothy at the end of Loch Glencoul. With a visit to Handa on the way.

Summer in the Summer Isles. The only change in the weather was that the rain, which had been falling nonstop all night, was now sheeting across in a force four north-westerly rather than coming down vertically.

There hadn't been a breath of wind the previous evening and, to avoid the midges I'd camped on a tiny island no bigger than my garden at home, just two patches of greenery rising above lichened and seaweed-covered rock. A few hundred yards away rose the larger islands of Tanera Beag and Fada Mor, but that stretch of sea was sufficient for

quarantine from the ravenous hordes, while a midge-hat kept off the few indigenous beasties. One of the great things about kayaking is that rain is no bother, you're dressed for wet anyway and I simply kept all my gear on till the tent was up.

The Summer Isles. What a name! Who can resist going on one of the island cruises widely advertised in Achiltibuie and Ullapool? Most tourists just land on Tanera Mor, walk the few steps to the post-office and cafe, then get back on the boat. Those islands had intrigued me for many years, now at last I'd enough experience and knowledge to manage a two-day trip under my own steam.

It's a long, tortuous drive to Achiltibuie from Caithness. The road passes through that amazing Assynt landscape of isolated sandstone peaks, some of which I hadn't climbed since I was in my teens. So I couldn't resist stopping to nip up little 2000-foot Stac Pollaidh, an irascible ridge of rugged pinnacles and towers probably, because of its dramatic appearance and easy access from the road, the most-climbed

A great skua on Eilean Dubh, one of the Summer Isles, with a view towards Coigach

scree-slopes have now been bypassed by a well-made path which climbs steeply round to the east of the main ridge with growing views over the magical Assynt landscape.

I don't recall any major difficulties on this ridge when I last climbed it from the north at the age of 18. But the crest is more like the Cuillin, with quite a bit of airy scrambling and lots of those dead-end paths made by lost walkers going the wrong way. The final scramble to the summit, exposed with a big drop below, I didn't quite fancy this time... after all, this was a kayaking trip! I was back down in little over an hour, the legs nicely stretched before spending hours cramped in a small boat.

My aim was to visit as many of the islands as possible in the two days, all the weather charts suggested very light winds though the inshore forecast hinted at a 'perhaps force six later'. Compared with the Pentland Firth, these are relatively benign seas with few problems of tides and big swells. My target for the first day was Priest island, one of the remotest at some seven miles out, returning to camp on one of the

Storm beach, Priest Island

more sheltered inner isles.

From a grassy sward near Achiltibuie I paddled out past Tanera Mor and across three miles of open sea towards Eilean Dubh, my designated lunch spot. The sea was gently rippling in a force three from the south, skies were grey but cloud was lifting off the mountains giving spectacular views of the rugged peaks of Coigach, An Teallach and Fisherfield. Approaching the island I could see a fine house just above the stony beach, it was occupied and to land there would have been like stopping in somebody's front garden. Instead I landed in a bouldery cove just to the west, and scrambled up to the 300-foot summit. These islands are not low and grassy like Orkney or Stroma. They are little bits of the western highlands

A view across remote Priest Island

to Ullapool ferry passed to the south. But I had the island to myself, for a rough climb to the highest point and a view over an interior of lochans and heather. I didn't linger too long, there was a long way to go, but could still savour the atmosphere of this remote spot.

Little Glas-Leac Beag, a couple of miles to the north, was my next staging post, I hauled out over barnacle-covered rocks – shaving yet more plastic off the boat which after three years is starting to look very battered – and walked up to the low island crest through the vegetation of angelica, mayweed and lovage growing on a soil of guano and seal droppings. Midges were swarming even on this tiny isle, I'm told the females can lay their first eggs without a feed but if they drink some blood can manage a second crop. Hence their suicidal attacks, they have nothing to lose. Do they attack the seals, which had been lying out before I landed? Twenty or thirty yards of sea was enough to get away from the insects. It was now flat calm, good for paddling but not for camping! A lovely, gentle

thrown into the sea, tangles of deep heather and tussock and rock, hilly with broken cliffs and lochs, very rough country. Coasts are rocky with some higher cliffs and the odd cave, but nothing like as severe as we're used to in Caithness.

Priest Island looked a long way off, but by hopping from island to island there were no long crossings and the wind was dying down. I'd push on, past Carn Iar and Bottle Island and over two miles of open sea to land on a steep storm beach of piled boulders as the first of the drizzle came on. This being August, there were quite a few boats around, a small yacht was just leaving the sheltered bay, earlier a RIB tourist trip had powered across in front of me and later the blue and white Stornoway

Looking south from Glas Leac Beag

Clearing skies, Tanera Mor

Horse Island, looking towards Coigach

crossing led past the steep angled rocks of Stac Mhic Aonghais, saluted by a pair of porpoises, and on round Tanera Beg, inspecting a couple of arches and caves. I'd planned to camp on this large island but chose my midge-free islet instead, paddling across the short channel the next morning to explore some of Tanera Beg's rugged landscape in the soft, blowing rain. The island was once grazed by sheep and quite recently burnt, old paths still remain giving slightly easier going.

There's a whole archipelago of little islands here, shores of tangle and rock, lovely easy paddling, the only exposed stretch being the northern tip of Tanera Mor in a choppy force four from the north-west. Lots of practice in rougher conditions on lochs and off the Caithness coast paid off, otherwise I'd have had to wait for the wind to drop or face a difficult portage across the island. Tanera Mor covers a couple of square miles, again largely rough moorland and rock, but with an inhabited eastern fringe around the big bay of the Anchorage – now a busy fish-farm. Perhaps a dozen houses, mostly summer homes or holiday cottages, are linked by a narrow and very wet path through lush vegetation and low trees. No roads. Fraser Darling cultivated some of the land during the 1940's and wrote of his experiences in his book 'Island Farm'; all trace of his efforts has since vanished. Nobody was about in the driving drizzle, but as I explored inland, pushing through deep wet heather to the island's summit at 450 feet, the weather was changing fast. Back at the boat the sun was already out, the clouds were lifting, one of those sudden changes typical of the west.

The wind was dropping away, so rather than a quick paddle back to the car I headed south for another two miles to Horse Island, now idyllic in warm sunshine with clear views of the soaring mainland peaks. I climbed to the top of Meall nan Gabhar, the vegetation almost entirely wild flowers and sat enjoying the sun and the stunning landscape. It was hard to imagine it was the same day I'd greeted nine hours earlier with heavy rain, cloud almost down to sea-level and visibility of half a mile. Just another three miles

or so of sunlit paddling remained, along the coast back to the car, with a bonus of warm sunshine and midge-free breezes to sort out all my wet stuff and pack up for the long drive back to Caithness. Summer had returned to the Summer Isles.

Island bound – setting out from Skerray on a fine day

Chapter 5   The Heart of the Far North

Footprints, maybe a fox, across a frozen lochan on the Knockfin Heights

Bog Ashphodel near Sordale

A flow-country loch

From the coast, the farmland and crofts of Caithness and East Sutherland run up into the famous flow country, a vast area of deep blanket bog sprinkled with lochans and dubh-lochs. Various tracks cross this landscape, some are estate roads and others remain from the disastrous 1980's attempts to turn the peatlands into commercial forestry.

A few years ago an estate bulldozed a track from Glutt Lodge right up to the crest of the Knockfin Heights, following the line of an old stalkers' path. The track ends just three straight miles from a forest road coming up from Forsinard, giving an obvious challenge for a mountain-bike crossing. My route would follow the track from Loch More to Forsinain, take the road to Forsinard then turn off onto that forest road which climbs up to the headwaters of the Halladale. From there I would wheel the bike up over the moors to pick up the Glutt track then pedal back to Loch More via Glutt and Dalnawhillan.

So, early on a morning of sunshine and hard frost, I pedalled down the Altnabreac track from the Loch More road. The soft surface was frozen hard, giving excellent cycling, the potholes easy to avoid. Beyond the frosted-white heather the waters of Loch Gaineimh were calm under the pale blue sky with the Caithness hills, still bearing a few streaks of snow, in the distance. On, through the endless forests of spruce and lodgepole pine, to Loch Caise. Here a public walk round the lochs was made with public money – but Fountain Forestry, who built the road from Loch More at the taxpayers' expense, do not

Sunset, Loch Stemster

Winter dawn, the beech avenue, Stemster

Summer on the Knockfins

Loch Thuim Ghlais

Rainbow at Hilliclay

An otter eating a rabbit at Loch More

Shurrery Loch

The Dunbeath Strath

Waterfall, Skelpick Burn

Obstacles!

allow the public to drive along it to the start of the walk. Crazy. On up to the railway and along the road to Altnabreac station, where some very tame stags took a while to saunter off as I approached. The forest road crosses the line then wanders around a bit, it was built to serve those notorious 1980's flow-country plantations which are now being cut down to restore the peatlands.

Indeed the only good legacy of that infamous diversion of taxpayers' money is this fine track, which now, without the surrounding trees, gives tremendous views across the high flow country before dipping down, taking a few more

twists and turns and climbing up to its highest point on the crest of Slettil Hill. Another good place to stop and admire the vast moors of Caithness and Sutherland spread out under the quiet late-winter sunshine. Then a fast, bumpy descent all the way to the River Halladale.

By now a light south wind was picking up, slowing progress back up the road to Forsinard. The river was low, very blue under the bright sky, early larks were singing, the road empty bar one or two delivery vans. The RSPB staff at Forsinard all seemed to be working indoors at their computers, there

weren't many birds about yet on the flows other than the occasional golden plover staking out its territory and already making its evocative calls, with the odd grouse or raven. Indeed there was nobody at all about on a day which was better than most in the summer.

A high locked gate on the forest road meant lifting the bike across it, I thought forests were supposed to be cycle- and horse-friendly! Then, half a mile on, a second locked gate really was overdoing things. Beyond these obstacles the track was easy, climbing steadily before turning up the valley above the upper Halladale. Here is the

Dawn across Loch Caluim and the flow country

Hope plantation, spruce and pine growing on peat right up to the 1000-foot contour. I call it the Faith, Hope and Charity forest – planted in faith with the hope that the trees might one day give an economic return at the charitable benevolence of the taxpayer. One has to admit though that after only 25 years some of the trees are already 15 feet tall.

The track crosses the Halladale and turns back north, there is an easier cross-country route to be had by following it to the end, then crossing the moors south of the railway.

Instead, I prepared for a couple of hour's hard slog. Wheeling the bike proved a bit less difficult than expected with the ghost of a quad-bike track to follow until I was stopped by a high forest fence. Once over this, the banks of the Halladale, now just a moorland stream, gave reasonable going to a fork, where a hint of an old route led up into the moors. No doubt many drovers and others came this way in the past, sometimes former drove routes are still visible as faint grassy or stony strips in the moor, also here were a couple of grass-grown piles of stones, the remains

The road to Shurrery Lodge

My trainers after a run over Morven...

was why I gave the otter such a fright, it ran across in front of me into a pool, splashed through, climbed out and made off down one of the headwater streamlets of the Thurso, its dark hide and long tail glistening wet in the sunshine.

It took nearly three hours from the Halladale before finally lifting the bike across the last ditch onto the end of the stony Glutt track. From just a couple of miles below the summit of the Knockfins this route follows the valley of the infant Thurso for some five miles down to Glutt, it would make a great trip to cycle all the way down the river from here to the sea. Or maybe kayak the stretch from Loch More.

It's a fun track to cycle, very stony, up and down, crossing and recrossing the upper Thurso and giving an easy route through this superb scenery of high moorland and rocky stream with the sharp triangle of Morven straight ahead. A magnificent, circular shooting hut has been built a mile or two down the track, complete with gas-fired barbecue and a wonderful view across the valley. Increasingly rough going

of old shielings.

Not many bicycles had been this way. Any sign of track vanished into typical Knockfin country of peat-hag and dubh-loch. A case of dragging and carrying the bike, trying to avoid the deepest peat hags but not always succeeding. The moors lay vast and silent under the dazzling sun, no sign or sound of mankind at all. Perhaps that

Mist and deep snow, Hilliclay Mains

Looking south from Olrig Hill

hammered the bike for the next few miles before finally emerging on the quiet river flats west of Glutt. Nobody was about, not even any dogs, it seems that the lodge is now left empty in the winter.

All I had to do now was pedal the ten easy miles down the good track to Loch More in the late afternoon sun. Could I get through Dalnawhillan without ringing the bell? Changing up a gear and standing on the pedals I gathered speed towards the kennels and gaggle of geese and hens outside the keeper's house... but as always every dog started barking furiously, the geese honked, the hens cackled, and everyone within three miles (which may, of course, have meant nobody) knew I was passing.

Further on, the keeper was burning heather, flames licking right up to the track and a pall of thick smoke to pedal through. Yes, it was muirburn time! Beyond, Loch More lay blue and still as the sun went down. It had been a good day, and a good route, two crossings of the Caithness flow country with only about three miles out of 45 on tarred roads, on perhaps the finest day yet of the year.

That unique and wonderful landscape of the flows does suffer from the fact that, if you are not following a track, the tussock, bog and deep heather give slow, hard going on foot. Under a blanket of snow it is even tougher, a knee- or waist-deep wallow – unless you are on skis. Then, you can make fast progress into the heart of the country and reach places that would otherwise, in such conditions, require a helicopter or a desperate slog.

The high plateau of the Knockfin Heights is one of my favourite destinations on a fine snowy day, providing the road to Forsinard is clear and unlikely to be blocked before evening – once I very nearly got stuck

West from Olrig Hill

North from Olrig Hill

when unexpected heavy snow came on during the day.

So on one of those beautiful crisp days, with temperatures way, way below freezing, I'd skied across the moor from the Forsinard-Kinbrace road and climbed, with some effort, up onto the plateau. It is amazing that nobody else ventures into such a wonderful place on such a day. Miles and miles of pristine snow, easy cross-country skiing with gentle slopes and frozen dubh-lochs. Mostly no sign of humanity at all, just occasionally a glimpse of the mast above Forsinard or of the concrete trig point on the summit of the Heights. You could be in the middle of Siberia or northern Canada, a dazzling white landscape stretching to a far horizon of snowy peaks. Stop and listen. Absolute silence. Nothing at all, no bird, animal, car. Not a breath of wind, with a thin haze of mist across the plateau where very cold air has pooled. Then the distant rattle of the train, crossing the County Summit, miles to the north. The hot sun on the snow gave a very faint scent, like ozone. Then came a sudden whiff of heather, an unexpected

Loch More

Loch More

Loch More

The Broubster Lochs   Loch More and Ben Alisky

evocation of spring in the winter landscape. A peat-hag was exposed, dark in the white expanse, absorbing the warmth of the sun.

The Knockfin Heights in winter are a lot wilder than even the Cairngorm plateau where you hear the constant whine of machinery drifting across from the ski-centre and there are lots of other people crossing to Ben Macdhui. Here, you are the only human for miles.

Cross-country skiing is reckoned to be one of the best forms of exercise, in spite of very low temperatures I was sweating most of the time and glad of a big flask of tea to rehydrate. Skiing on, over frozen loch and tussock, progress was much faster than it would be on foot in summer. A pity there was nobody to pick me up at Braemore, that would make a good through route, instead I had to turn round and head back north. There were very few animal tracks in the snow, the deer were all down near the road. A single hare had ventured up near the summit, and the tracks of a fox purposely headed in a straight line, east-west. Grouse had landed and hopped about, here and there excavating deeper hollows in the snow to reach buried heather, before wingprints showed where they had taken off.

In the midst of the plateau, is a little wooden post with some cryptic numbers and letters inscribed. I call it 'The Lost Post', it's probably something to do with some RSPB wildlife survey, this whole area is, in world terms, an extremely special and almost unique place.

I managed to ski down gentle inclines towards the valley without falling, an otter too had been enjoying several hundred yards of downhill sliding by a stream gully, leaving marks

Looking towards the Griams from the Knockfin Heights

Looking towards Morven and Scaraben from the Knockfin Heights

Winter scenes, flow country

The summit of Ben Alisky

Over the moors from the Griams

Sunset at Hilliclay

The Loch Dubh hut

like a child's sledge interspersed with footprints where the animal had lolloped to the top of another steep slope.

A week later, and even more snow. Another good opportunity to ski into the heart of the flow country, this time from Loch More. I hadn't visited Ben Alisky for years, this low hill is about six miles west of Loch More and a bit of a slog through the bog on foot. It always made a good destination when doing training runs for the Highland Cross, returning along the Dalnawhillan track.

In the early morning I made fast progress on skis across frozen Loch More, keeping close to the shore for safety, before heading up over the moors from the far end of the loch. Knowing well how rough and wet these moors are, it was great to ski easily over all the difficulties, hard work but a steady rhythm of slide with the legs and push with the arms, Ben Alisky slowly drawing nearer. Northwards, the only sign of life was the dark splash on the white landscape of the buildings at Dalnawhillan and, yes, those kennelled dogs which bark furiously when you pass could be faintly heard a couple of miles away.

I took a diagonal route across steeper slopes then turned back

The River Forss west of Dorrery – the track to Loch Caluim crosses here, I call this spot the Gateway to the Flow Country.

THE HEART OF THE FAR NORTH

The memorial plaque to Stanton Avery near Loch Dubh

door just as a heavy snow-shower drove in. The hut had been warmed by the sun and I sat drinking tea and eating a sandwich as the snow whirled outside, the visibility shrunk to ten yards or so. Some seven miles from the nearest road, the only way I'd have reached this place in deep snow was by ski. A note on the wall welcomes visitors to this out-of-the-way spot and asks them to sign the book, there can only have been a hundred or so signatures since the hut was erected ten years earlier. Amazingly, it was nearly eight years since my previous visit.

As the snow-shower cleared and blue sky began to appear again I set off up Beinn Breac to the west, skiing easily up slopes now covered by another half inch of fresh snow. On the summit is a stone memorial to the man who owned the Dunbeath estate in the late 20th Century and did much to preserve the landscape for posterity. The plaque reads:

'I intend to initiate and support efforts to explore, study, preserve and maintain the prehistoric and historic sites and structures of Dunbeath in harmony with the ongoing

northwards as the view opened out to the Knockfins and the high peaks of Morven and Scaraben, soon gaining the summit with its big, well-constructed cairn.

A mile to the south, in the middle of a totally white landscape, was a black dot. That would be my next objective. Gentle slopes gave an enjoyable descent to Loch Dubh, frozen and deeply snow-covered. Briefly the wind picked up, helping me along, and a few pellets of hail blew past as I skied across the frozen loch. The black dot had now resolved itself into a small wooden hut, as I approached I saw a little veranda and a double door, welcoming me into a small cosy room with windows looking out over the empty landscape. I scraped away the drifted snow and opened the

Sheep at Hilliclay

contemporary life of Dunbeath Village, the crofts, the grazings, the fishing, the grouse moor and the deer forest.' R. Stanton Avery, Laird 10 August 1976 - 1 May 1997. 'If you seek his memorial, look around you'.

If only the current estate owner would follow those aims instead of seeking to desecrate the heart of this magnificent landscape with a giant wind farm. Stanton Avery must be turning in his grave.

Northwards now, an easy glide to the old settlement of Benalisky, ruins of a later shepherd's house almost buried in drifted snow. Here too is an old corrugated iron hut, it must be stronger than it looks as I always expect to find it demolished by storms. But still it stands, and only a few hours' work would be needed to make it a habitable shelter again.

Cross country skiing is indeed hard exercise, and it was still six miles back to Loch More. I aimed directly for the distant dot of Backlass and hoped that the snow hadn't softened too much in the sun. There was, though, no hurry, and with occasional stops for more tea and sandwiches, I could enjoy crossing this normally very rough country with relative ease. The Allt Backlass is often a problem, not wishing to wade its icy waters I had to detour upstream for about half a mile to where it splits; I balanced across one of the two tributaries on the skis, and leapt over the other. A small herd of deer had been scratching in the deep snow for grass and rushes, I caught up with them above Backlass. Normally you envy the deer their ease of running over rough country through which you painfully slog, now it was the deer that wallowed in snow two feet deep while I skied easily over the top of it. They would be hungry and weak, I did my best to avoid disturbing them.

Even the normally easy track to Backlass was deeply drifted over, only near the road-end were there any footprints of walkers. A small group of people had come out to see the sun

The ruinous Thulachan Lodge, now lost and forgotten in the heart of the flow country, was once equipped with hot baths and flush toilets.

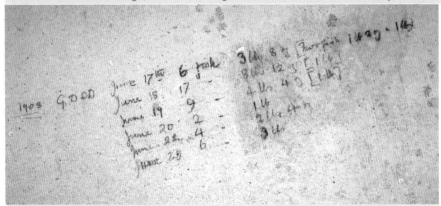

A fishing tally from 1903 written on one of the walls inside Thulachan Lodge.

places in Britain wilder than Loch Dubh or the Knockfin Heights in the middle of winter.

going down over the white landscape, for somebody from the city even this accessible spot must seem like the heart of the wilds. There are though few

Loch More

The track from Glutt Lodge

Chapter 6 Around Whiten Head

The 'Dougal' rock stack and Whiten Head. Loch Eriboll

Whiten Head from the south

'Impracticable to all but the hardy and active native, to him even it was a day of toil and labour.' So reads the plaque on the old Moin House, recording the state of the country prior to the construction of the road in 1830. The house, built for the shelter of travellers, now stands roofless, defaced inside by the kind of ugly graffiti more associated with cities. The old road has been largely bypassed by the new, but still gives a good route on foot over the top of the Moin between Loch Eriboll and the Kyle of Tongue. I was jogging, never having run the route before even though I'd cycled it many a time. June – and an east wind, 10C, fingers of grey mist licking the moors and cold driving rain. Good Moin weather! I love this place, spectacular in rain, spectacular in clear sunshine with outstanding views of the high Sutherland peaks, the old road runs right past lochans with red-throated divers wailing. It's ten miles from Ard Neakie on Loch Eriboll to the Tongue Causeway and it took me longer than it should have done.

The cliffs around Whiten Head form, in my opinion, the finest stretch of coastal scenery in the north of Scotland. In a land of superlatives, that is something. The remoteness helps, few trek the rough and pathless miles to visit the area. The area teems with wildlife, grey-seals pup in large numbers in the autumn, badgers, wildcats, golden eagles, ospreys, deer, foxes, all inhabit this country. Views south over Loch Eriboll to Foinaven and Ben Hope are stunning, sunsets spectacular. Midges and clegs can swarm in numbers you'd not believe possible. Although once inhabited it's now a truly wild place, inhospitable and beautiful. Hopefully, the sacrilegious suggestion of a vast

A fine morning, Ard Neakie, Loch Eriboll

A perfect day for a paddle, Loch Eriboll

The 'Crooked House' on Ard Neakie, now sadly collapsed

super-quarry immediately across the loch, south of Durness, has gone away.

Although I know most of that coast very well indeed, it's only in the last few years, after taking up sea-kayaking, that I've been able to explore from the sea. The opportunity for my first trip came one fine September day. Shortly after eight I paddled out from the lime-kilns of Ard Neakie into a gently rippling Loch Eriboll under a brilliant blue sky, with a forecast for easterly winds of no more than force three. It has been said that to kayak from Elgol to Loch Coruisk and back, on Skye, is the best one-day paddle in the world. A round trip from

Sgor a' Bhaic

Looking south from Freisgill

Ard Neakie to Whiten Head must come a close second.

My first target, two or three miles to the north, was the rocky island of Sgor a' Bhaic. The coast of Loch Eriboll here consists of low cliffs and grassy slopes, there's a little lighthouse above a prominent outcrop of quartzite looking for all the world like a big splash of white paint. This part of the loch is well sheltered, I paddled gently to conserve energy but made good progress and within 45 minutes had beached the boat in a little stony bay on the tiny island.

Hardly more than a rocky skerry, completely washed by waves in storms, the narrow crest bears a covering of tussocky grass. Black-backed gulls fussed at this rare intruder.

On my way again, a following wind picking up to make little crested waves, I made a beeline for the cliffs below Freisgill, a couple of miles further on. I'd explore this part of the coast more thoroughly on the way back, first I wanted to visit some of the spectacular scenery of stacks, arches and caves towards Whiten Head. It was strange to

see a coast I knew so well from a very different perspective. Rounding the Freisgill headland, the rock stack I've always known as 'Dougal' came into sight (it resembles the 1960's 'Magic Roundabout' canine character of that name) with the inaccessible grey seal bays behind. Inaccessible from the land, that is. A sea-cave, like a tunnel, took me straight through a little headland to the sheltered bay of tangle and rocks basking in the sun between Dougal and the mainland. Another two big caves took me back through the stack then

Looking over Loch Eriboll to Foinaven from Freisgill

The 'Dougal' stack from the sea

Uamh Fhreasgil, looking towards Spionnaidh and Cranstackie

out again into the bay, I paddled on round towards a rock in the open sea where a huge bull seal was resting, it slid into the sea as I approached. These big animals sometimes make a very unnerving splash, always just behind the boat – but are never aggressive in the water, after all a human in a boat looks, to them, much bigger than they are! The swell was picking up as I paddled on, but there's a very fine natural arch just short of Whiten Head and who knows when I'd have another opportunity... it was too choppy to risk a photo of the towering arch as I paddled through and immediately turned southwards again for more sheltered waters. From land that arch is an unsettling place with a flat grassy sward like a bowling green suddenly giving way at a crumbling edge to a vertical drop into a usually-boiling sea.

By now, feeling very hungry, it was time for a break, I paddled into the bay below Dougal and landed among seaweedy boulders on the stony shore, to enjoy some sandwiches and a flask of tea in a stunning setting of blue sea and

The big arch and the crumbling cliffs above

sky and soaring cliffs. I noticed another sea-cave leading through the cliffs at the northern end of the beach, this gave a good route out before heading south for Uamh Fhreasgil, reputedly one of the longest sea caves in Britain. There are many dark, sinister-looking sea-caves which I don't fancy exploring on my own. But this is a big, open cave of red-and-white rock into which the light streams, sheltered from the swell I could paddle in about 300 feet to where the waves lapped on a small stony beach in the cool, seaweed-scented, sea-cave air. The entrance framed a lovely view of the Foinaven hills to the south. Even this friendly cave wasn't though a place for the nervous, with echoing booms as swell surged into some hidden crack and huge splashes as seals crept up behind the boat in the dark and suddenly dived.

Landing again on the big quartzite pebbles below Freisgill, I walked up the hill for a second lunch, sitting in the sunshine to admire the tremendous scene and enjoy the great peace of this quiet corner of Scotland. There's so much gloom and doom about these days, so much stress and worry and trouble – it does a great deal of good to remind oneself that places like this still exist, the grey seals and the badgers and the bothy mice get on with their lives regardless of cuts and conferences and cancers as the sun rises and the sun sets and the quiet bothy watches the seasons turn.

More cloud to the south over the hills heralded a gradual change in the weather but the wind was still only a light force three and I had all afternoon

Freisgill bothy with Eilean Hoan and Cape Wrath beyond

Eriboll sunset

The 'toothpaste rock'

to explore the coast to the south. Huge piled boulders tumble steeply into the sea below the cliffs south of Freisgill, I could imagine the effort it would take to follow that coast on foot. There was a very small

Loch Eriboll from Whiten Head

The stacks from Whiten Head

Grey seal pup, Freisgill

Looking south from Whiten Head

The Waterfall Cave, Loch Eriboll

seal, its head showing out of the water – then it dived and I saw a tail. An otter.

I've known The 'Waterfall Cave' for over 30 years. Countless times I've passed the spot when walking out along the cliffs towards Whiten Head. The Allt an t-Strathain, draining the high peat moors of the Moin, runs into an attractive steep-sided valley of bracken and heather, before plunging over a 30-foot (or so) waterfall into the sea. The river needs to be forded upstream of the fall, and is sometimes impassable in spate. To get a reasonable view of the waterfall from the land is not easy or recommended, you have to scramble down a steep and loose slope above a vertical drop and only then do you realise that, behind the lower part of the fall, is a sea cave.

Now from the boat I could see a white veil of water running down the cliff and over the low entrance of the cave to splash into the sea. It was possible to paddle in, beside the fall, behind was a shallow cave with a stony beach. I could look out through the

The Whiten Head stacks

falling water to the sunlit loch. A passage, at the side of the cave, led through to a second cave with a different exit to the sea, this place must have been well known to the select few in the days of clans and smugglers and illicit stills! Onwards again, rounding the high cliffs below Goat Hill, crossing the mouth of the River Hope to land in swell washing onto on a lovely little

sandy beach just to the west. I don't like just paddling for hours, preferring to frequently land and explore, I'd never been to this beautiful little bay before and don't expect it sees many visitors.

Dark cliffs and caves led on southwards, the loch intermittently choppy from a variable wind. Rounding the lighthouse again I paddled up the middle of the loch, straight into dazzling

warm sunshine with the mountains round the head of the loch ahead. Eilean Choraidh, low and green, beckoned, a mile to the south... but that was really enough for one day. I paddled round Ard Neakie to land on the south shore, as a freshening south-easterly rippled the loch and the mountains basked in the late-afternoon sun.

A more serious trip I'd been planning for a while was to paddle the entire stretch of those wild and remote cliffs north and west of Melness, rounding Whiten Head. Only the Cape Wrath coast is more demanding, there are high cliffs, few landings, and some 20 miles of paddling before reaching Ard Neakie. Twice I'd had the trip in mind – and twice decided it was too daunting.

On the first occasion a forecast of increasing north-west winds gave me the excuse to head for the more sheltered inland Loch Hope, a superb stretch of water, over six miles from the bridge at Hope Lodge to the birch woods below the steep ramparts of Ben Hope. The loch is much favoured by fishermen seeking trout or sea-trout but also makes a fine, safe paddle along its rocky,

A sandy beach near InverHope, Loch Eriboll

Arnaboll

Loch Hope

wooded and moorland shores.

Mist and rain hung over the loch as I set off from the Altnaharra road opposite the white building of Arnaboll, once a township. The loch shores were well populated until 1820 when the people were evicted in the infamous clearances. Behind Arnaboll is an old graveyard, maintained by the council until the 1970's though the last burial was probably 70 or 80 years ago. Coffins used to be carried over an old path from Kembie on Loch Eriboll. The building at Arnaboll is now looked after by Durness Primary School as an outdoor centre in a truly delectable setting, it's an easy mile's walk down a grassy track through the woods from the main road.

In quiet drizzle I paddled up the western shore of the loch below tumbled boulders and birch woods to within sight of Hope Lodge, then turned and headed south. A more peaceful journey is hard to imagine, the road on the far shore sees few vehicles, not even one motorbike disturbed the quiet, just the occasional distant puttering of an angler's outboard motor. Empty moors and stony shores slowly passed, the rain gradually dying out, the cloud still low, veiling Ben Hope. A clump of trees on an 'almost' island marks the southern end of the loch where the Strathmore River flows in. Turning north again I landed to stretch the legs by nipping up the 1700-foot An Lean Charn, a rocky top I hadn't visited for years. The cloud gradually lifted, clearing the summit as an eagle coasted the length of the cliffs. Steep crags dropped away towards Loch Eriboll with the long Durness road a ribbon round its slabby shores.

A late autumn day, Kyle of Tongue

A deer fence on the western side of Loch Hope encompasses several square miles of totally failed native tree plantings. Upturned divots can still be discerned, a few displaying dead twigs and perhaps one in a hundred bearing some stunted leaves. Deer are inside the fence, maybe the wrong strains of trees were used, overall it's the most useless forest I've ever seen – planted of course with our money.

By contrast the native trees on the eastern side of the loch are doing fine, it was a lovely paddle along bouldery shores below the woods, swollen burns rushing downhill into the loch, the first hints of autumn colours and that evocative scent of birch and dying bracken. Weather was clearing from the north, sun appearing, the wind still light – maybe I'd have managed that sea paddle after all. But there was always next week.

Indeed a week later gave a perfect morning with a slight frost and clear skies. Just the usual south-east wind picking up in the afternoon. An early start from home meant I was again paddling out from Ard Neakie into the smooth waters of Loch Eriboll shortly after eight as the low sun glowed on the white rocky slopes of Spionnaidh, Cranstackie and Foinaven. Breakers coming into the Kyle of Tongue, combined with the prospect for rising winds – only 10 mph according to the forecast, but off-shore south-easterlies

The Whiten Head flag poles

Mol Mhor, below Whiten Head

on a fine day usually get a lot stronger than that – had already decided me to keep to the relatively sheltered waters Loch Eriboll.

Ninety minutes later, and I was paddling in towards the stony beach on Eilean Hoan (burial island – a burial site used by the Norse) just east of Durness. I'd passed little Eilean Cluimhrig and paddled through its sea caves but found too much swell to land, the green Eilean Hoan looked much more attractive. In the morning sunshine I wandered round this quiet island of grass and a few grazing sheep, it's leased by the RSPB and is an important site for wintering Greenland Barnacle Geese. Remains of former settlements were everywhere, old lazybeds and field boundaries, the low walls of a long house, overgrown stony mounds. Limestone protrudes through the grass, this must be a superb spot for wild flowers. An uninhabited island all to myself on a glorious sunny morning – the freedom given by a paddle.

Freedom to set off for Whiten Head, less than an hour across to the high headland but many miles and hours round the loch by land. The semi-circular bay of Mol Mhor with the white cliffs towering 600 feet above was perhaps the most impressive spot I'd yet visited by kayak. Indeed quite daunting, dark in the shadow, a force four south-easterly now making the water choppy, adding to a gentle swell rolling in from the west and breaking on the rocks and boulder-beach. I'd have landed but the grey seals were there before me, the first of the white pups, born in the autumn, were lying with their mothers among the stones.

Through caves, in and out of rocky bays, round sea-stacks and geos I paddled, in sunshine and shadow, seals splashing in the water and singing from the bouldery shores. Two huge bull seals were fighting head to head by a waterfall

The high sea cliffs east of Whiten Head

East towards Port Vasgo

The highest cliffs

tumbling onto the rounded boulders. I'd been paddling straight into dazzling sun reflecting off the water, overpowering in spite of sunglasses and sunhat, I hadn't anticipated sunburn as a hazard at the end of September. The last two miles were hard, directly into a force four, I'm still surprised how winds which I wouldn't normally even notice make such a difference to the kayaker. The tide was low, rocks covered in seaweed exposed below the cliffs, near the shore I could see I was actually making progress. At last, the stony beach at Ard Neakie and the car parked just beyond. The sun still shone, perhaps it really was the last day of summer.

It was indeed to be the following year before I finally managed that twenty-mile paddle round Whiten Head, it gave some of the toughest paddling I've yet encountered and made a real little expedition. The forecast was for slight seas and light south-easterly winds, picking up a bit more from the east the next day. Rain was likely but of no concern in a boat, I'd have the tide against me for much of the way but preferred a following wind. I left the car at the cemetery near the Kyle of Tongue causeway and launched the kayak. Initially it seemed almost too easy. The sea was glassy, the skies mostly grey with a few light showers and the odd gleam of sun. Snipe circled with their 'squeaky-wheel' cries, a couple of distant cuckoos called. My first destination – the Rabbit Isles, was an hour or so's paddle down the Kyle, the only hard work a brief fight against the current off the Talmine sands. The head of an otter broke the surface near the island shore,

The area of rocky coast and little sandy bays occupying less than a square mile around Port Vasgo really deserves more than just a quick visit, early July gave probably the best display of wild flowers I've ever seen. We went for a look and ended up spending the whole day just exploring the meadows, clifftops and beaches of what I'd thought were just a couple of bare headlands. Indeed these grassy areas have just enough grazing to keep the long grass down but not too much that the flowers suffer. To the east, west and south are the normal heather and peat moors of Sutherland, just here is the short, flower-rich turf of the clifftops.

Wild thyme, with its fresh scent of the high mountains, has always been one of my favourites and here the grasslands were liberally sprinkled with big patches of the tiny purple flowers. As we crossed the headland towards Stac Mor, we saw the first Scottish Primrose plant. And another. And another. The ground was speckled with the diminutive plants, just a couple of inches high sporting their cluster of little pink flowers, almost growing like daisies. Some of the plants

seals surfaced and snorted and splashed. I pulled the boat up onto the sandspit joining the two islands and had a brief walk up to the hilltop, wishing I'd given myself more time as the wild flowers were lovely, squill, campion, primrose, orchids, kidney-vetch to name a few. A short-eared owl took off from amid the sand-dune tussocks, a strange bird to see circling over the sea.

That sandy beach joining the two islands is one of my favourite places and I'd always wanted to make a journey which involved hauling the boat across the narrow strip of sand and setting off again from the far side. Here it was a little more choppy but nothing to worry about, past Dubh Sgeir Mor and Eilean Chaol, helped by a gentle breeze round the headland, passing Port Vasgo to land again on a little sandy beach just west of the point. I'd planned this trip as a hop from bay to bay, not wishing to paddle for hours on end. Ahead was the committing part of the trip, many miles of exposed coast below high cliffs.

The vertical cliffs of An Stac

Flowers at Port Vasgo – Water-lily, Scottish Primrose, Thyme, Lesser Butterfly Orchid

step, every fresh headland brought more meadows into view.

Loch Vasgo – a lovely display of white lesser butterfly orchid on the shore – with white water-lilies floating in the water and tall pink red-rattle among the white tufts of bog-cotton by the water. The wet ground was thick with the red, sticky leaves of long-leaved sundew and its tiny white flowers, the more rounded leaves of the short-leaved variety on drier ground. Here too were fine clumps of yellow bog ashphodel, growing among the pink of cross-leaved heath and red-purple bell heather, with many scattered spikes of heath orchid, white and pale pink. Almost the only rarity we hadn't seen was mountain avens, with its little oak-like leaves and white, eight-petalled flowers, and this grows profusely on the grassy limestone slopes of Ard Neakie among the thyme-scented grass.

I doubt that there is any designation to protect the Port Vasgo area, few know about it or go there. With global warming or change in land-use, who knows for how long it will be possible to enjoy such an amazing natural

had as many as seven flowers, there were hundreds of them, never have we seen so many growing in one place. Here too the bright blue milk-vetch, the everlasting, and a pink parsley-like flower later identified as sea-carrot.

White bladder campion and thrift crept over the rocks near the cliffs, with large, tumbled patches of yellow kidney-vetch. A little clump of red bearberry hung off a shady rock. There was fleshy rose-root growing down the cliffs, there was purple lousewort and blue milkwort and yellow trefoil and Scottish thistle. Swathes of yellow buttercup – then another surprise, a large patch of the beautiful globe buttercup with its big, almost spherical yellow flowers. Every

Landing on the bays under the high cliffs

spectacle? How do we protect and preserve such places without the red-tape and keep-out attitudes which characterise so much of conservation? I don't know. Perhaps one just has to hope that the local owners and crofters wish to keep the landscape as it is.

Now I stopped at Port Vasgo just long enough to munch some early sandwiches, the sky looked brighter to the west, maybe it would turn into a lovely calm sunny day for pottering along, exploring the sea-caves and arches and beaches. Alas no. A sudden

unexpected squall blew across. The clearance was a weather front, with associated winds, but I reckoned it wouldn't last so set out across the bay into the choppy waves. Indeed clear it did, and the sun came out – but the wind, ignoring the weather forecast, remained obstinately in my face. No more than a gentle force three, but there's a world of difference between paddling into a force three and being helped along with the wind at your back. The tide and the swell were also against me, it would be a slow paddle. I

consoled myself with the knowledge that paddling into the waves is safer than having a following sea.

I've walked along the top of these spectacular cliffs, rising to 800 feet, many times. Several high waterfalls tumble into deep, rocky bays. Stacks rear up. And is it ever calm? The sea was as choppy as any I've paddled in, the swell bouncing off the cliffs giving confused water mixing with smaller wind-driven waves. An hour of this and I was glad to reach a boulder beach under the high cliffs, thank goodness for

The Whiten Head stacks

plastic boats which stand up to the battering of landing on boulders in waves. A bite to eat, then summon up strength and set off again, for the next stage round the 600-foot rock headland of An Stac.

Another hour's paddle and a tiny shingle beach surrounded by the high cliffs. Waiting for a break in the surf I managed to land at the western end, quickly leaping out of the boat and hauling it up out of reach of the waves. A truly amazing spot, probably unvisited from one year to the next, wet shingle gleaming in the sun, views of high waterfalls and of the soaring cliffs of An Stac. I'd have appreciated it more if it wasn't that the crux of the trip, Whiten Head, was still ahead. In another break in the surf I launched again, paddling just east of the high cliffs which gave some shelter. The stacks of Whiten Head are less well-known but almost as spectacular as those of Duncansby, yet dwarfed by the towering cliffs above. They gave some shelter from the wind and waves, once round the headland I'd be on the home straight for Freisgill bothy, where I planned to overnight. There was no turning back now.

The sea always surprises. On my previous visit, it had been relatively calm out to Whiten Head from Eriboll and I'd turned back before much rougher seas around the stacks. Now, as I rounded the headland expecting better conditions I found the hardest paddling conditions of the day. Probably a combination of a tide running out of Loch Eriboll meeting a swell and waves and wind all from different directions, bouncing and reflecting off the cliffs, gave a completely confused sea with lumps erupting into spray from all sides. If I'd been out with the club, the leader would no doubt have said that this was nothing, only sea condition two and wind force two, any beginner should cope fine! But there was nowhere to land, nobody to rescue me if I fell in.

And slow, as much time spent bracing as paddling, no opportunity for the luxury of feeling tired or losing concentration. I hardly noticed the boulder-bay of Mol Mhor under the 600-foot white cliffs, or the big sea cave just to the south, or the clifftop rock which looks like toothpaste extruded from a tube. But the boat was coping fine, slow progress was made, gradually the sea eased off a bit. Ahead the big stack of Dougal, a brief chance to relax in calm sheltered water in the bay to the east, but the tide was low and there was no exit to the south other than through a big cave back out into the breaking waves. Just another mile to paddle, not even looking at the fine sea caves, and at last a landing on the rocks below Freisgill, very glad I didn't have any further to go that night.

For once another group was staying at the bothy, gathering whelks, I hardly saw them as they were in late and off again at 4am for the next low tide. It was a lovely sunny evening but I was shattered after the long day and in my sleeping bag not long after eight. The night was fine and calm, but by morning

cloudy and soon raining again. At least the forecast was right this time, with a freshening north-east wind giving an easy paddle up the last five miles of loch to Ard Neakie. It had taken me perhaps eight hours of paddling round the coast, not counting stops, and over two hours to jog back to the car along the road over the Moin. It felt strange to then drive in less than 15 minutes from the

Tongue Causeway to Loch Eriboll to pick up the boat. What would those who built the early Moin road have thought of that?

Chapter 7   The Isle of Stroma

Cliffs of West Stroma

The much-photographed old church

Old font by the church

Stroma. The island in the stream, surrounded by immense tide races and wild seas. Now uninhabited, Stroma lies just two miles off the Caithness coast and is a frequent subject of articles, pamphlets, photographs, paintings, even books, with the many empty, ruinous houses a particular attraction. The people left, willingly, in the 1950's for a better life on the mainland, some using money they had earned building the new harbour. The melancholy aspect many people impart to the place is largely romantic nonsense. Stroma is now run as a large farm, with regular visits by the owners for all the necessary tasks involved in looking after sheep and cattle.

It is though strange to visit what was once a densely populated island and have the whole place to myself. Though you may not be as alone as you think. Once I was just heading back past the old church to the harbour when a voice called out 'Hello Ralph' – it was a lady I knew who with her husband, a former native of the island, was staying in a renovated cottage for their annual three-week break on the island

Stroma is now a haven for wildlife and flowers, long may it remain so in this age of windfarms and tidal turbines. Many others have written at length about the island, so it is the wild aspects I'm going to concentrate on here.

To paddle alone around Stroma in a kayak is often regarded as an exacting trip requiring high levels of qualification and experience. Choose a day with one

Stroma Beacon – in typical Stroma weather?

The narrow slot below Castle Mestag

The remains of the wrecked *Danika* before further storms left little remaining

of the smallest tidal ranges of the year combined with calm seas and light winds and, provided you get the timing right, it's hardly more difficult than a paddle round Thurso boating pond (nevertheless don't try it alone unless your sea kayaking ability is at least at the 4-star level!)

I set off from Gills in the afternoon, just after the ferry had left for Orkney. The west-going ebb tide was dying away, I would be round the north of Stroma before the Swilkie whirlpool built up on the east-going flood. The sea was flat calm, the sun hot, the strong tides of the Inner Sound subdued to almost nothing. Soon I was off the Stroma Beacon and heading up the west coast. Many years ago the 'Danika' was wrecked here, ploughing at speed into the cliffs. The remains of the boat are still lodged in a geo, to salvage all the valuable bits and pieces a ship gangway was used to bridge a narrow gap to a large sea-stack above the boat. Once, the stack housed Castle Mestag, probably a base of the notorious pirate Sweyn in the 12th Century (and later owned by the Sinclairs), there would then have been a drawbridge in place of the makeshift modern bridge.

Between the high rock walls of the castle stack and the mainland is a long

Stroma Harbour

The Gloup

Through the Gloup

famous 'Gloup', a cliff-rimmed basin in the moor. A few weeks earlier the RIB '*North Coast Explorer*' had been wrecked here when her rear thrusters failed while taking tourists into the entrance of the cave, her passengers and crew had to be rescued by the Thurso lifeboat. Now, with only the smallest of swells, the spectacular high-roofed tunnel gave an easy paddle through to the boulder-beach surrounded by cliffs which I'd only before visited from the land. The wrecked boat had either been salvaged or had sunk, only a faint smell of diesel lingered.

I've seen the tide-race here like a raging river, now just a gentle current helped me round towards the lighthouse, though choppy waves were already starting to build as the tide strengthened. A little more effort was needed against the eddy to make it into the lighthouse pier just to the south. As I lazily enjoyed some food and a flask of tea in the sunshine, the '*Pentland Venture*' sailed up from John O'Groats packed with tourists enjoying the afternoon wildlife cruise, she sat offshore for a few minutes while folk watched the

narrow passage, barely wider than a kayak, amazingly the sea was calm enough to paddle right through. Beyond, the usual Stroma swell and tidal eddies were almost non-existent, allowing a gentle potter up the wild western cliffs. Grey seals lay out and swam in their hundreds. They would quietly gather behind me till 30 or 40 heads were swimming after the boat, the occasional animal finding it was too close and diving with a loud unnerving splash. If I looked round, they would gently submerge, one by one. Others slept, heads just above the surface. One only woke when I could nearly touch it, rocking the boat and spraying me with water as it dived right alongside.

Near the north end of the island is the subterranean passage leading to the

Looking down into the Gloup

Grey seals near the lighthouse

Looking across the Firth to Dunnet Head

A view to Swona

This rusting tractor is a favourite target for photographers!

By the lighthouse

East coast

Walking on the water – a 'Brocken Spectre' produced by my shadow projected on mist above the sea.

Tide race near the Swilkie

Sentinel oystercatcher

The lighthouse pier

Noise

The *Pentalina* on her way to Orkney

The Kennedy mausoleum, Scarton Point

too hot so, perversely, landed to put on my waterproof cag so that I could find a sheltered inlet and enjoy half a dozen rolls to cool off. There are those who reckon you don't need to learn to roll a kayak, perhaps on safety grounds you don't, but it's a great playful thing to do on a hot day! Nicely cooled off, I set off for the hard journey back to Gills with the tide against me, waving goodbye to the seals lying out on just-submerged rocks by the Beacon. Pointing the boat south-west and paddling hard, my course ended up just east of south with the tide trying to carry me back past John O' Groats. Just like crossing a wide river, with big smooth boils of water and circular currents around. I wonder how the 400 tidal turbines to be installed here by 2020 will change things, especially with all the maintenance boat traffic. Once across and out of the tide, an easy two miles past Canisbay Church took me back to Gills in the early evening where cars were queueing for the next Orkney ferry.

At the end of October the kayak was washed and stowed in the garage, the gear cleaned and put away.

unconcerned seals then headed back the way she had come. There were other visitors to the island, three quad bikes came roaring down the old road and earlier I'd seen a small group of folk watching seals from the clifftops. I jogged up to the top of the island for the stunning view of sunlit islands and blue seas, then back to the lighthouse to see that, neap tide or no, the Swilkie had built into that mass of churning white which small boats are well-advised to avoid. No, you shouldn't attempt to kayak round Stroma unless you really know what you are doing.

Tidal currents were mostly weak though and it wasn't a hard paddle down the eastern side of the island and along the southern shore past the harbour. In the beating sun I was much

The island road

Off Scarton Point

November and December are not usually good months for sea-kayaking. Then came an amazing fortnight of almost Indian summer weather, light winds, mild...

So perhaps a late season, last paddle around Dunnet Bay would still be possible. A few years ago I tried this and spent the whole of a precious afternoon taking the boat down to Castletown, getting dressed up in all the gear, capsizing twice trying to paddle out through the swell, then packing everything up again and going home. The one thing I don't like about sea-kayaking is the time and hassle it takes to actually get into the sea, properly equipped, and then to get back home and wash and dry the gear. I have a checklist, in my old age, to make sure I don't forget anything important and it runs to 44 items ranging from 'boat' (yes, I could even leave that behind), to VHF radio, to having checked that I've allowed for the

difference between BST and GMT on the tide-tables.

The morning was grey with a stiff offshore wind, I paddled out of Castletown harbour and headed across the bay for Dwarwick, good practice trying to keep a straight course with choppy waves coming at me from the side. Very peaceful, a few eider ducks and shags and one or two very small black-and-white birds on the water which might perhaps have been storm petrels (but I've never claimed to be a bird-watcher...) It looked too rough to

Newly hatched gull chicks

carry on towards Dunnet Head so I simply turned back, paddling slowly into the wind along Dunnet Bay and doing a bit of gentle surfing in the two-foot waves breaking on the sands. The beach was empty, not even one dog-walker on this grey November Monday morning. 'Always practice your roll, even when going out in winter,' say the books. I plucked up courage to submerge a couple of times in the uninviting-looking cold water near the harbour and decided to do the rest of my winter practicing in the swimming pool.

Once again I washed the boat and put it away in the garage... and the quiet weather continued. For various reasons it was the end of the settled spell before I could get out again. Overnight rain was going to clear to a fine calm sunny morning but with the wind picking up from the south in the afternoon. The tidal range was average. A rare chance for a winter trip to Stroma. Sea conditions were forecast as 'rough' but this simply means a big swell and the Inner Sound is reasonably sheltered from the west, moreover with a harbour at both ends of the crossing there would be no need for surf launches or landings. Slack water at around eight in the morning meant that if I could get organised to set off early from Gills I'd have an easy paddle across, the west-going tide would help me back later in the morning. That timing also made sure I kept out of the way of the *Pentalina* ferry which can take a route on either side of Stroma on her journey to Orkney.

Nevertheless, a solo crossing to Stroma at the end of November was not something I'd attempted before, and it was with some trepidation that I paddled out of Gills in the growing light of dawn. It was much cooler than it had been, clear sky was advancing from the west while above and to the east thick high cloud remained from the weather front which had cleared through

Grey seals by the road

overnight. The west-going tide would start picking up in less than an hour and that ferry would be coming, incentives to paddle hard aiming for the eastern corner of the island, two miles away. I needn't have worried about sea conditions, just a gentle rolling swell and small choppy waves on a light southerly breeze.

Tidal current atlases and tide tables are wonderful things but I still only half-believed the forecast of no strong tides and kept well away from big waves breaking off the Stroma Beacon and along the western side of the island.

I paddled into the harbour, looking forward to landing as usual on the stony beach. I'd forgotten the grey seals. It was late in the breeding season and many would, by now, have taken to the sea. But there were still at least a dozen pups of various sizes on the stones, some with adults beside them and even a bull seal making amorous advances on one of the females in the water. Where to land to avoid disturbance? The slipway from the inner harbour basin was fortunately largely clear of the seals, though a couple of well-grown pups snarled from the top as I pulled the

boat up. Others, well camouflaged against the grey concrete and stones, hissed. They have a nasty bite, best watch where you're putting your feet! I changed into jogging clothes and set off for a quick look round the island. It was not yet nine, but I'd have to set off back across no later than 11-30 to be sure of missing both the rising wind and the Pentalina on her second crossing from the Hope.

The cloud gradually cleared eastwards to leave brilliant, low sunshine illuminating the views of islands and sea and coast. Many grey

A view across Stroma

nobody on watch. The crew were safely rescued but the boat could not be saved.

I jogged on along the higher cliffs, admiring the big waves breaking with the sea surging through the tunnel into the rocky bowl of the Gloup. North of the lighthouse, the Swilkie was churning white, the west-going tide meeting the big swell coming from the west. Beyond, sun glowed on Swona – an island I've yet to visit on the other side of the main channel of the Pentland Firth, a case of so near and yet so far. Time was getting short now, so back by the old road across the island, past the empty houses, school and church. On this northern part of Stroma the seals had taken over. A mother with a white pup lay in the middle of the field east of the road, at least 200 yards from the sea. Two well-grown pups splashed in a pool by the road under one of the ruined cottages. Others lay in fields above the shore, among the grazing sheep. It felt like one of those TV programmes about a world where all humans have suddenly died. The wildlife is taking over, 50 years after the people left.

This boat was wrecked in Autumn 2011

seal pups and adults lay on the stony beaches to the west of the harbour but quite a few had ventured further. Some pups lay on the grass on top of the low cliffs, with 'seal paths' leading down to the rocky geos along which the adults had slithered. Here was an adult pair, male and female, in the grass at least 100 yards from the sea.

Waves were smashing through the narrow passages by Castle Mestag where I'd paddled in still water three months earlier. Further north, a wrecked fishing boat lay firmly aground on slabby rocks, pounded by the surf. The 'Golden Promise' is not the first boat to have run straight into the island at full speed in calm weather on automatic pilot with

In the clear sunshine, with the old buildings casting long shadows and the far peaks of Sutherland sharp under a brilliant blue sky, it was a shame to be heading back so soon. But I'd already stolen a march on late November and didn't want to push my luck. The southerly breeze was increasing and indeed the sea off the harbour looked quite choppy with the tide now flowing rapidly westward.

So, carefully negotiating a route to the water between the seals, I paddled out of the shelter and pointed the boat towards John O Groats, I really did not want to be swept into the rough conditions around the Beacon. The sun was low and dazzling off the sea, I'd brought a floppy hat and sunglasses knowing that the north of Scotland can be a suntrap at the end of November but even so it was mostly with one eye shut that I paddled hard south, straight into the sun, across the huge river of sea flowing west, letting the tide take me towards Gills.

Stroma thrift

Stroma tysties

Looking back, the island of Stroma basked in the low sun, as enticing as ever. But the boat was soon safely back in the garage and there wouldn't be another chance to visit before next Spring!

Stroma west coast